Zero To Hero

Nate Wilson

Preface

As an addict, I thought of myself—and was treated by society—as a zero. A nobody. A degenerate. Every addict has a story—and a hero inside who was damaged on the streets or when using.

In recovery, I think the only way to be successful is to treat yourself exactly as that—a hero. I didn't recover just to become an average Joe or just to work an average job and hide my story from everybody. It took me awhile to see it, but I am a hero. For years, even during my recovery, I thought of myself as a degenerate, almost sub-human. As I continued in recovery, grew stronger, and started connecting the dots to my crazy life, I realized I have potential to be a hero. I want to share my story to inspire people. If my story of hope saves even one life and I can be a hero to someone, then the evil of addiction in my life will have been redeemed for good.

Table of Contents

1. Just an Ordinary Kid

2. High School Blues

3. Becoming a Young Man . . . and a Bigger Addict

4. Psychosis and Going Over the Edge

5. The Moment of Truth

6. Recovery . . . and Alcohol

7. Finding Success and Peace

This book is dedicated to the all of our loved ones who have passed and no longer have a voice to share their story.

This book is also dedicated to Mr. Krajcovic, the crazy old creative writing teacher who told me I would be a writer one day.

Introduction

This can happen to anyone. All of my stories, my crazy decisions. The path and whirlwind of addiction. It can happen to anyone. I had everything and every opportunity to say "no" to the lifestyle I chose. But it didn't happen like that.

Growing up, I had great parents who loved me and gave me everything they possibly could to give me a good life. I played sports, went to church, and had plenty of friends. When I was in grade school, I thought strongly of God, and I prayed a lot. I was an only child, so I felt I had to grow up to be an all-star. My father showed up to all my sports games and even coached me in baseball through high school.

I liked being a class clown in middle school, and I liked attention. On the flip side, I also had a very private and introverted attitude at times. I was good at sports, though, and also was making big hits in football even though I was small. I recall one game when the coach called me out in front of the whole team to congratulate me on playing like I was bigger than I was.

I played baseball, and my family treated it like a religion. I got to go to Cooperstown, New York, to play with some of the most talented in the country. It was the experience of a lifetime. On the outside, everything was fine. My family was living the "American dream." But on the inside, something inside of me became hurt and tainted.

Addiction to meth had no care or regard for what my parents plans for me were or even what my plans for my future were. The drug sits and waits for the most unsuspecting of people. Young or old, brown or white, male or female, smoking or snorting, it doesn't matter. Its evil sits inside the baggie and waits for its next victim—and anyone is a sitting duck. All it takes is one time to steal your ambition—your life—and change you to your very core. From the second I tried the drug, I was changed on a molecular level in a way I can't explain. Meth will disguise itself, too. It will use your talents against you. If you choose meth, you may get high and be so stimulated that you perform better at sports, or write a paper better, or have a profound thought process you think can't be touched. But it's a lie.

I recall a time in high school when I chose to get high on meth and stay awake all night to finish a paper in creative writing. I excelled in creative writing and English. The next day, my teacher told me that one day I could make money off of my writings if I continued to write as well as I did on that particular paper.

That spark doesn't last long though. The happy cells get depleted, and the sleep deprivation adds up. A few years later, I was strung out and had been up for days with a pen and a pad writing myself into an oblivion of nothingness, wishing I could remember what sparked me to write as well as I did when I was 16. My talent became my weakness.

Meth distorted my thinking, and my writings made no sense at all because of my meth-induced psychosis. Sports were no longer an option because I had no physical stamina, nor the ambition to play. Even seeking therapy for my emotional problems had become nearly impossible; I had no practical way to communicate who I was or what I was feeling because of my poor mental state. And to think I used to be so "normal".

That's part of what made recovery so hard. Looking back at how structured my life was before meth, I lived about 14 years as functional as possible, but within five years of using drugs, I had been completely brainwashed from the streets and from drugs. I had no idea who I was. My good childhood memories were blocked out; I had forgotten what made me ME!

My quest in life is to pick up those broken pieces and formulate a new version of myself. From the moment I decided I wanted to change, I've had to teach myself how to be a better me. How to walk, how to talk, how to think like . . . ME! If I can do it, anyone can do it.

Chapter 1

Just an Ordinary Kid

Listen to the mustn'ts, child, listen to the don'ts.
Listen to the shouldn't, the impossible, the wont's.
Listen to the never haves, then listen close to me. Anything can happen, child, anything can be.

— Shel Silverstein

I'm sitting in a graveyard, next to two dead friends. No wait, three dead friends, and another one about 50 yards away. I feel safe to cry here, and I haven't cried like this in years. Damn, it feels good. I've been holding this toxic feeling for years and years. "Seven years clean, and my brain still lacks coping skills," I say to myself. I say it to whoever is listening. I say it to God. I say it to my dead friends. I say it to some supernatural force that lingers in this cemetery in hope of some mercy or pity. It's different when you're sober and you can feel. The pain is real, and there is no escape. I haven't been drunk in a month and it takes every ounce of persistence and better judgement not to stop by the liquor store. Drinking may be easier and temporarily better for stability, but I'm changing . . . I don't want to leave the cemetery, but I have to go home . . . I have to continue changing . . .

This whole breakdown at the cemetery was started by what I consider a really small ticket from a cop: "Expired registration, and no proof of insurance." A week earlier, I awoke as the proudest man on the planet. I was proud of marking my 7th year without drugs and one month without alcohol. And now I'm in a graveyard crying over a ticket. This is something that wouldn't have fazed me a few years ago, or especially seven years ago.

There was a day when having my head slammed into the wall by ATF agents and being taken to jail didn't slow me down. I see my weakness and I need to grow. I told myself in the graveyard, in the midst of my breakdown, that if I saw a cop I would punch the accelerator to the floor and run my car off of a cliff before I would pull over again. On the way home, I decided to calm down. I'm glad that night is gone. I'm laughing at this as I write. Not because of how sick and crazy I may be, but because I am triumphant.

Only a week later, and I am better prepared and becoming a new person from that. When I reflect on my conquered struggles, it fills me up. Something from the inside moving out. I get a small grin on my face that I can't control, and my eyes tear up. I close them, and my thoughts slow down. Peace. For a few minutes, I feel like myself. I feel like I'm using all of my spirit and everything is in tune for once. My vision is no longer hazy. If I can sustain this feeling for long enough, I can remember how I felt before all the drugs and before the heartache. Unfortunately, this is not always my reality. Even in recovery, this is a rare moment of clarity for me.

The Beginning

My story starts in Woodland Park, Colorado, a small town that lies about 30 minutes west of Colorado Springs, where I was born, at Memorial Hospital on February 23, 1988.. I am an only child to a loving father and mother, Wes and Julie Wilson. I grew up in the same house my whole life, in a nice small-town subdivision. My early years were mostly normal and spent playing sports, being coached by my dad, going to church on Sundays, and hanging out with friends that lived in my neighborhood. My parents were deep into the church congregation and very insistent on me being involved as well. I can recall going to church up until about age 16, willingly or unwillingly, just about every single Sunday, participating in youth group and any other church activity that was available to my age group. My parents wanted me protected from the harshness of the modern world. No explicit music or movies, strict curfew, keeping tabs on who I was hanging out with, random shakedowns in my bedroom. I was different, though. I was a free spirit. I questioned things all the time. More eccentric, but sometimes the opposite, and more introverted. Sometimes I liked trouble, too. I can remember acting out as early as third grade, when I started stealing horror books from the library. My friend and I were obsessed with vampires, monsters, and horror movies. As an adult, I realized there may have been a reason I began to act out. There was a "sore" in the back of my mind that festered as it stayed in the dark. With time, as the sore went unaddressed, this caused me to act out more, almost as if I was trying to distract myself or others from what was really going on inside of me.

Total Recall

When I was 27, I had a conversation with my father that sparked a question: "What was my earliest memory?" From the time I was 18 to about 27 years old, I had the hardest time recalling childhood memories. From drug use? Yes, maybe a little. But it was more than that. I believe it was from an emotional detachment. My refusal to remember good things like who I am and what made me . . . ME! An ignorant choice made in my subconscious to remain broken.

At 28, I decided it was time to be myself and explore my first memories. Two things came to mind. I recall one night being in the car with my father, my cousins, and my uncle. We were on our way to Seven Falls to see Christmas lights. Seven Falls is a tourist attraction that comprises seven beautiful waterfalls in Cheyenne Canyon, in the foothills west of

Colorado Springs. I was the youngest, and my older cousins were teaching me to count to 100. I remember lots of laughing and conversation. It was dark, and I would normally have been home getting ready for bed, but I was still out and about, and it made me feel older and adventurous. My first experience of bonding and feeling love and attachment to someone. I don't remember seeing the seven falls, but I do remember my family. I remember my first adventure.

While recalling that euphoric night spent with family, another memory came to mind. It was a recurring memory of something that had been weighing on my heart for several years. I can't recall my age, but I remember what I felt like. I spent my days playing with one or two kids from the neighborhood and spent the rest of the time with my mother and father. The world was big and brand new, and at my fingertips.

There was one girl that left a big impression on my childhood—my babysitter. She had become a close friend to the family, lived next door, and her parents were friends with mine. Her mother was a plump woman with shaded glasses and short, curly, black hair. She was always nice to me. Her stepdad had strawberry blonde hair and was plump as well. His cheeks were always red, and he never smiled or said much. My babysitter had an anxious type of movement about her, like she was rushed all the time or like she was running from something.

One day, she took me into her bedroom and sat me down on the bed. The room was dark, as the time was getting late and the sun was setting, leaving a shade of blue in the room. Once again, she seemed anxious, rushed, like she had something burning inside that she wanted to tell me. She asked me if I had ever French kissed before.

I started to tell her no, but before I could complete the word, her lips made her way to mine, and her tongue forced its way into my mouth. Dazed, I felt the smooth texture of her tongue on mine, and the swirling of hers around mine made me dizzy. Each movement of her tongue stunned me more, until I couldn't move. She backed off for a second, and I sat speechless. She leaned in for another kiss, and our breathing got heavier. There was more touching and so much going on my brain felt like it was going berserk.

The house shook, and a door slammed. Her parents were home. She pulled away, put her index finger up and said, "Don't ever tell anyone about this!"

So, I didn't. The sternness in her voice set the tone and programmed my brain to never question what had just happened. Everything happened so fast, but lasted for what felt like years.

I went home and pretended to forget. I blocked this out most of my life. It was dark. It was a violation. It was a dirty feeling. It was an embarrassing memory. It was a shameful feeling for me. It was a burden passed down from her to me. If I had talked about it at an earlier age, maybe I would have been a different person, but I had no capability of doing so. I would watch the "good touch, bad touch" movies in school and never once considered myself the one they were trying to reach. I wondered how many of my elementary school peers sitting around me had been molested. My mind put the memory of that dark room, with the lights off in the darkest and quietest part of my brain. It literally didn't exist in my conscious mind, and life went on. Each day passed, and I buried it just a little more.

I held the secret well. Years later, as an adult, I wondered how much I was affected by my babysitter's sexual violation of my young body and mind. I wished I could have seen the lie I was living by remaining silent. What would have happened if I had confronted and confessed the molestation? Would I have been a different person? Would I have had proper instruction and counseling? A life without addiction? Who knows?

During my drug-using years, it was apparent to me that most of the people I associated with had no concept of reasoning through problem-solving or a sense of normalcy amid pure chaos. It was evident to me that they grew up with pain or dysfunction they believed to be normal. These were red flags: signs of neglect and environmental risk factors that lead to addiction.

Early in my addiction, I was told by many that I acted more mature than others and more functional (at first). They said that I was the least crazy junkie out of anyone they had met. On one hand, I attributed this to my parents' example of social behavior that was set for me. On the other hand, I blamed them for some of my frustration and internal anger because I felt smothered from them as well.

Environment vs. Genetics

[1]No single ingredient triggers someone to become an addict, only long recipes that boil down to a molecular level. You don't have to grow up in a completely miserable childhood to be a drug addict. I was not an oppressed child. Genetics also play a part.

Everyone's brain is wired with a rewards system in it. We observe this in animals with their food. The advantage to this is that when animals eat food, they are rewarded with happy cells in their brains. This causes craving and initiates the will for them to search for food and stay alive. This is advantageous and a survival instinct as well.

We observe humans abusing dopamine in their brains every day, whether shopping too much, overeating during the holidays, playing too many video games, or overworking. Regular overindulgence of an activity to receive relief or "happy" feeling is addiction. The brain releases the chemical dopamine to be sent through the brain circuits to produce that happy feeling. It is believed that those who become addicted do not produce a normal level of dopamine—and other chemical secretions of the brain, such as serotonin, oxytocin, and endorphins—even before they try drugs, and their brains crave more of that drug after the first dose.

During drug use, the flood of dopamine is so high that this can make it nearly impossible for the brain to recycle enough of the brain chemical to be used again. After the euphoria—or "high"—goes away, the addict is left with a chemical imbalance and a lack of "happy" cells and dopamine. This is why cravings happen. The chemical imbalance also includes anhedonia (the inability to feel pleasure) and desensitization, which is diminished emotional responsiveness to a negative, aversive, or positive stimulus after repeated exposure to it.

The flux in the brain's function with chemical imbalances indicate that _every_ human has the potential to become an addict. Those people with low chances of addiction, genetically speaking, may still develop an addiction through overuse of the "rewards" pathways in the brain, basically rewiring that system.

But not everyone is dopamine deprived. Those who are not dopamine deprived, the ones who do _not_ become addicted, typically feel

---

[1] http://bigthink.com/going-mental/your-brain-on-drugs-dopamine-and-addiction

uncomfortable under the influence of a substance and may experience panic attacks, feel out of control, or feel paranoid.

During the time I was on the streets, I noticed that people who had somewhat normal childhoods and upbringings—with exception of me—didn't crave drugs like I did. I would often be the bad influence on friends, getting them to try hard drugs once and noticing that they didn't crave it like I did. They would seem to have a good hold of their emotions without the need for drugs.

On the contrary, an addict will feel comforted under the influence. Some claim the drug made them feel, from their first use, like a hole was filled in their emotions or they felt "normal" for the first time in their life. I can relate to this feeling, from the first time I smoked meth from a bong.

Genetic Predisposition?

[2]Is there a connection between childhood trauma and chemical imbalances? We know genetic predisposition exists. It can be observed in some ethnic groups, such as Asian or Jewish, or the stereotype "If you're Irish, then you're a drinker." That stereotype may hold some truth to it. Some Asians experience the "Asian flush" when they drink, which means that their heart rate increases, their faces may turn red, and their liver does not metabolize acetaldehyde (a chemical born in alcohol consumption) the same as others. It can cause vomiting and extreme sweating in some cases. The factor that would cause someone to take the first step and try the actual substance is another subject.

It's impossible to say what gene activates addiction, but research suggests that genetics play only half the role in addiction. Other research shows that environment also plays another big role in addiction risk. [3]In 1970, in Vancouver, Washington, psychology professor Bruce Alexander conducted an experiment using rats and drugs. He tweaked a previous experiment in which rats were placed in a cage alone with drugged water and regular water. The rats chose the drugged water and eventually killed themselves. Professor Alexander changed the scenario for these rats and placed them in a much more desirable environment with colored balls, quality rat food, lots of recreational equipment, and other rats to be around. The rats tried the drugged water and the regular water, but these rats did not take the

---

[3] http://www.brucekalexander.com/articles-speeches/rat-park/148-addiction-the-view-from-rat-park

drugged water. They chose the healthier water and lived prosperously in "Rat Town," while other rats in their lonely environments became heavy users and either died or lived addictively.

The result of this experiment suggests that the genetic risk of addiction can be swayed or decreased when a person is in a loving and supportive environment versus an environment that lacks nurturing. [4] Scientific studies claim that genetics play one half of the role in creating an addict, with environment and/or poor coping skills being the other half. If an adolescent begins to use drugs, this may be an indicator of underlying problems in his or her environment, but environmental factors do not mean this person will turn into an addict.

Risk Factors

For instance, 14 is the age I started to use drugs. I chose to succumb to my environment. It was common in my school and in my circle of friends. I was in middle school, but many of my friends had older high-school siblings or friends who used drugs. The drugs in the high school environment trickled down into my circle and seeped into my environment as well. I tried drugs once because I was familiar with them being in my environment, and then I continued to use because, I believe, my brain chemistry is predisposed to being an addict. Knowing what I know now, I can almost picture what my brain's dopamine receptors looked like.

Despite coming from a supportive household, I still had environmental risk factors: the molestation by my babysitter coupled with peer pressure. And, despite my parents not being addicts or alcoholics, I could still have the genetic chemical imbalance or childhood trauma that correlates with uneven brain chemistry.

---

[4] https://addictionsandrecovery.org/is-addiction-a-disease.htm

[5]To think that if my drug addiction was kicked off only by having drugs in my school environment and just a spark of curiosity, what would be the odds for someone who grows up with drugs or alcohol in the household every day? A recipe for disaster. This is very common in drug addicts. They watch their parents, family members, or friends use substances day after day, programming the hard drive of their brain to normalizing substance abuse.

What makes me an addict? It was a perfect storm. I picture myself like a kid sitting on a teeter totter with just an ounce of imbalance—and a flick of the devil's finger, just enough to topple me over into a world of pain. [6]

Fear and Love

[7]It has been said that the two most basic emotions we feel as humans are fear and love. All of our negative feelings, such as anger, resentment, depression, isolation, are rooted back to fear. This took a while for me to grasp, but once I figured it out, it made perfect sense. Every time I was angry was because I was feeling defensive and fearful about my physical safety, my reputation, or loss of control over my life. The list goes on.

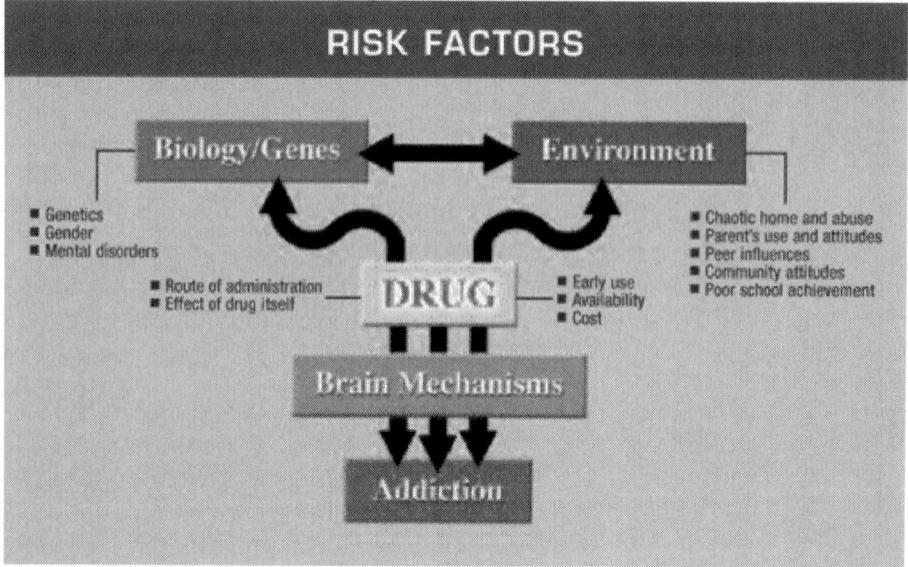

Whenever I felt depressed, I isolated myself from the world, because I

5

https://d14rmgtrwzf5a.cloudfront.net/sites/default/files/images/content/sciencefair_risk.gif

[7] http://www.abundance-and-happiness.com/love-and-fear.html

was fearful of what others would think if they knew the real me. They would see me as weak and prey on my struggles.

Fear drives unhealthy behavior, and it's difficult to think rationally when in fight-or-flight response mode—only impulsively. We all have painful experiences as children and as adults. Instinctively, we avoid these actions again. If we ride our bikes carelessly, we may fall over and break an arm. We learn to be more careful the next time and ride with caution. However, we have control over a bike. We don't have control over every aspect of our lives.

When we are young, if we are hurt by a family member—physically, emotionally, or both—we don't have control over other humans as we do while riding our bikes. Instinctively, we distance ourselves from others, not knowing whether they are a threat or not. We are driven by fear, and it can start at an early age for some. For me, it started with my early sexual encounter with the babysitter and may have worsened as I grew older. I lost trust in my parents and distanced myself from them more and more as I got older. I can see now where their frustration would come from. *If only Nate would listen to us . . .* But my trust wasn't there. Fear stood in the way. They wanted to protect me and watch me grow into the brighter side of the world. I didn't understand this. I had already been touched by the dark side.

I feared they wouldn't protect me and also feared they did not have my best interest at heart. It doesn't take a bad childhood experience to become a victim of fear. We all have felt it, and our society seems to perpetuate it. If you don't look a certain way, others won't accept you. If you don't listen to certain music, then you are abnormal. If you don't wear these clothes or watch those sitcoms or watch football, you are not normal. We do what we are told we should do out of fear, instead of rationalizing what is best for ourselves. Because of this, kids are cheating themselves out of their potential.

[8]The part of our brain that tells us to fear, our amygdala, starts to drive our decision-making instead of the frontal cortex, our rational thinking part of the brain. It's no mystery why younger generations aren't using rational thinking.

An addict's brain mimics this same paradigm. My actions were made out of fear of rejection, fear of being myself, fear of my secrets being

---

[8] http://www.resourceaddiction.com/amygdala-function-and-addiction/

brought to light. They started small, and I began to medicate them. At first, it worked. I felt invincible countless times. I felt more like myself than ever. But eventually, I would come down from the high, and the fears would return unsolved and now bigger because of the chemical imbalance. They turned into delusions under the influence of meth. Eventually, I couldn't hide them and exposed them to everyone. I felt bare. This was rock bottom. I started out with a few fears and ended up with a head full of spiritual warfare. My mind was a battlefield; it was literally pure chaos in my head. Not a second without doubt or paranoia.

So, what kills fear? Love

Think of a time when you could be yourself around someone and not have to wear a mask, someone you could reveal a deep secret to without fear. You have love for this person, or you love yourself enough to be confident in communicating with this person. Love allows trust, confidence, good decisions, and the ability to solve problems positively. Love allows us to accept the past and move on without regret. It allows forgiveness of ourselves and of others, even when they have wronged us.

Love is as instinctive as fear. When you love yourself, you can face fear head on. Just as we learn fear from pain, we learn love from being loved. I was fortunate to watch my parents love me as much as they could, which made it easier for me to find my way back when I was lost on the streets. On a chemical level, there are particular brain chemicals that are released when a feeling of love comes over us. Those chemicals include oxytocin, serotonin, and dopamine. These are the exact chemicals released in drug use. It's painfully obvious why drug addicts choose to take drugs.

Where there is no love, fear abounds, and the need for love, or the chemicals released that give us the feeling of love, is met in the synthetic chemicals from drugs. In a life that has been absent of these feel-good chemicals, the person finds comfort under the influence of drugs. When recovering from drugs, it's difficult to feel love because, chemically, there is little love to be had. Without the chemicals that are triggered with feelings of love, loving yourself is hard, but not impossible. These chemicals are just assets of love. True love is a conscious choice. When you are truly ready for recovery and ready to face your fears, you will overcome any obstacle in your way.

Choose Love

Choosing love doesn't extinguish fear. In fact, when you make the conscious decision to love yourself, your mind instinctively brings these fears to light, since you are now strong enough to face them. You can now choose not to react on your fears and look upon them rationally. This is why recovery is so hard. Some doubt themselves when their fears continue, which may trigger a relapse. Such vulnerability leaves us feeling the most fearful, with no drugs to medicate. It is a lot of work, but completely necessary. There's an old saying that comes to mind when I think of my early recovery: "Fake it until you make it."

This compares to my early recovery, because I literally did not have the brain chemicals to be happy or to love my life. There were times when I would force a smile when I didn't feel happy, and at times I would have to override my instinct to be sad and numb and force myself to talk. I forced myself to open up, even when it was ugly, with empty words. But I don't think I was faking it. I was *practicing* happiness. Or I was *creating* my happiness. I had forgotten what love and happiness were. My brain was too foggy, and my emotional trauma blocked my memories of love. But I knew it existed. I had faith. I pushed through the darkness with blind faith and practiced what I thought a happy person would act and be like. I forced myself to remember how I felt as a kid, what the freedom of being happy was like. I knew my thought process would be curved to this new philosophy. I didn't feel it inside at first, but, eventually, my mind caught on to my actions. My brain chemicals slowly came back. My words started making sense, and my memories came back to me. I chose to love myself, and I chose to love being sober.

Fear	**Love**
Instinctive	Instinctive
Creates Barriers	Drives Rational Thinking
Creates anger	Confident
Fight or flight	Forgiving
Rejects	Vulnerable
Causes low esteem	Accepts

Emotions and Spirituality

My childhood felt much more complex than love and fear. I thought of my spirituality and feelings as being deep and complex, and they were. But the roots of fear and love being the foundations was something beyond me. As a child, my brain had been programmed (or conditioned?) to believe that spirituality was something felt only by those who attended church. Those who didn't go to church I thought of as shallow, lost, or misguided on their spiritual walk. The truth is *this* philosophy was shallow. However, I also conceived an analytical thought process and deep sense of emotions through spirituality by going to church. I always looked for a deeper meaning in everything. Even when I was using or distant from my spiritual self, I believed that circumstances in my life were not by coincidence and had a purpose greater than I. I felt a deep connection to my emotions and was somewhat of a hyper-sensitive kid. I had a complex thought process through analyzing my emotions. My mother and father nurtured my emotions and gave me stability in times of trial.

Because of this sensitivity, I often took things to heart. I didn't understand superficial "shooting the shit" or small talk. I didn't understand that sometimes things are said for no reason but for entertainment or trash talk. This connection I had to my emotions guided my spirit, and my spirit guided me. With unsettled emotions, my spirit was frantically seeking comfort and peace, and was eventually fooled by drug addiction. I look back now and realize I was led by my emotions instead of logic, as I thought with my feelings.

I excelled in subjects in school, like English and writing, that allowed me to exercise my philosophy, and I strayed from subjects, like science and math, that enforced boundaries or rules. I wanted to believe I could walk through walls. That may be impossible, but my desire for it pushed me to be better. I was taught to have a big heart and to be dedicated to whatever I do.

This is how I describe my spirit. Spirituality is the unseen truth in every person. Your spirit knows every time you lie or fake something. It drives you when you are broken. To believe in your spirit, you must believe in something greater. This is not a Bible thump. Some connect to their spirit through praying on a mat, or even through snowboarding, whatever brings the feeling of a greater cause and a connection to a greater being.

I remember during rehab, I was taken to an Alcoholics Anonymous meeting inside the hospital on the bottom floor. There were a few old guys who showed us how to conduct AA meetings. Most had been in recovery for a long time. You can tell some of these men had been through the rough, and they weren't easy on the eyes; their faces told the story of their hard lives. One night, the topic of a higher power came up. One of the other kids from my group had mentioned how he didn't have a higher power, because he didn't believe in God. When his turn to talk was finished, an older man named Jeff chimed in.

"Jeff, alcoholic," he introduced himself.

"Hi, Jeff!" everyone responded.

He had a northern, Midwestern accent. He belonged in the movie *Fargo*. He went on for a minute about how a higher power isn't the Christian God most of us had been brainwashed to believe in. He brought up Charlie Brown and the Great Pumpkin. He went through the story about how Linus, though doubted by everybody, had stood tall in his faith in the Great Pumpkin. He wrote letters to the Great Pumpkin. And when he was shunned by everybody, he chose to keep it to himself, but never lost his faith in the pumpkin.

I watched as Jeff explained this story as if he were Linus. He lifted his hands to show the shape of a pumpkin. "Linus believed so much in this pumpkin, he fell asleep in the pumpkin patch in the freezing weather just to wait for him," he explained with passion.

He explained it in a way that made it so appealing to live so strongly for something. It was clear that he felt the same passion about his spirituality in recovery as Linus did about his Great Pumpkin. In that moment, I realized what faith and spirituality were. What a higher power is. Some call it God, some call it spirituality, some go to church, some snowboard, some play music—and Linus slept in the cold for his.

Spirituality is what drives you to sleep in the cold. It's something that you keep striving for in spite of everyone's doubt. It is different for every person, and if it challenges you to be a better person, then it's not wrong. There is a universal concept in every recovering addict that involves spirituality and believing in something greater and bigger in the universe. My spirituality started in an evangelical church and evolved through the chapters of my life into who I am now. My connections to my spirit have sometimes changed, but the fire is stronger.

With addiction comes a huge disconnect between spirit and body. Most addicts will testify to being disconnected from their higher power, or spirit. I can tell you, in middle school I disconnected from my spirit long before the drugs came around. I disconnected from my spirit when I focused on what I looked like through another person's eyes. I imagine most young people do. Even at six years old I experienced a huge disconnect when I decided to create a lie and block out my pain. I acted as though my emotions didn't affect me. My focus turned to figuring out what mask I wanted to wear each day or how I could fish for attention from others, even if it was negative. My inner child was slowly being shoved into the ground.

Ordinary

The rest of my elementary school days were considered normal. I was an active child who played sports, went to school, and stayed active in the church, even at a young age. My parents were big on me being in sports. I played baseball and football, and later got into skateboarding. I was coached by my dad in baseball and played in competitive leagues for most of my youth. When I was 12, I went to Cooperstown, New York, to see the baseball Hall of Fame and play in a tournament on a team with some of the best in Colorado Springs against some of the best in the country. This was the experience of a lifetime. I was given the nickname "Mr. Excitement" by the head coach, because of my quiet, calm, and seemingly unexcited demeanor. On the inside, I was having a blast, though, and it was one of the greatest opportunities I'd ever had.

I went to all the church outings, and I remember how they affected me. I prayed often and considered myself to be a good Christian boy. I remember how inspired I was by going to my church's youth conferences. They gave me a fire deep in my heart, and I felt I had God's favor. I felt so humbled and obedient when I would participate and act "godly." Since I thought I was in God's favor, I figured my dreams of wanting to be a professional athlete or a rock star would come true. I thought I would graduate high school, go to college, and marry my high school sweetheart. I was so young and had no idea what was about to occur.

I spent other days playing army with the neighbor kids and riding bikes. My best friend lived across the street and had a similar family structure. A few other families in the neighborhood went to the same church and shared the same religious belief system as my family. Things seemed to be as near to perfect as they could be. I guess it was a little too cliché' to be true. Things changed. My friends moved out of the neighborhood, and new kids moved in. My babysitter moved out of her house as well. Her mother was sent to prison for embezzlement, and the brokenness of their home became apparent to me. My guess is that someone in her life was hurting or molesting her, which would explain her approach to me. I found out that in a house down the street, about a half a mile away, another friend had been molested by his older brother. What was wrong with this neighborhood? Well, it wasn't just the neighborhood.

As I get older, I hear more and more stories of other kids who had the same or worse childhood experiences. I now know why my group of friends were attracted to each other: We all were hurting; we all tried to escape our realities. I see this every day in kids and even adults. "Degenerates." "Anti-social." "Convicts." "Lowlifes." "Outcasts."

They are none of those derogatory terms; they are broken people. The reasons are many, and they vary from person to person. They are the hardest to help, but they need it the most. I know this because I was one of those outcasts. I was lucky enough to have the foundation set by my parents so I could find my way back, even though I barely did. Not everyone has that, though.

I hope I can inspire this broken family of addicts and outcasts that I consider my own to find their way back to a healthy lifestyle. Getting clean has to be desired by the heart, understood by the mind, and driven by the soul.

Middle School

In middle school, I was somewhat of a class clown. I liked attention, and I liked to tell jokes. I made friends with as many kids as I could. I felt I had developed two sides to me. One was what my parents wanted me to be: athletic, liked by many, and social. And the other side wanted to be "bad" and rebel. I wasn't the biggest troublemaker, but—from sixth through eighth grades—I was temporarily suspended from school at least once a year for fighting. And there were more fights that I didn't get in trouble for. I wasn't especially violent; I just liked to get rowdy and run my mouth. In seventh grade, however, I did stab my friend 15 times with a pen after he punched me in the face. Looking back, this may have been excessive.

In eighth grade, a kid passing me the other way in the lunch room knocked me over and spilled milk on me. Instinctually, I stood up and started punching. My inner rage had been tapped. We exchanged blows;

then I turned to walk away. My friend Andrew yelled, "Watch out, Nate!" I turned around and dodged a straight punch. He left himself open, so I threw another straight right and watched his head click back as he fell to the ground. I didn't stick around, but I heard from a friend his nose started gushing blood and the teachers came to his rescue quickly. He identified me in the year book, and we were both given suspensions.

Unfortunately for me, I was not the toughest student. I can recall another time when a much bigger kid named Tyler gave me three quick jabs to the face after a dispute over a football game. Won some, lost some.

I discovered cigarettes when I was around 12 years old. My friends from down the street had parents who smoked, and I thought it was cool. This was my environmental factor. I tried it one day so I could feel cool and be accepted into the crew. I could ride bikes and smoke cigarettes with the older kids and the bad kids. After my first cigarette, I ran home for baseball practice and threw up my pizza. I didn't want to smoke after that, but I did anyway. I continued to smoke and eventually got caught when my mother could smell it. She lifted my fingers to her nose and her eyebrows furrowed—one of the most shameful moments of my life up to that point. This was my first taste of a controlled substance, and although I hated the taste and the smell, and even hated the effect, I continued to smoke my Newports.

My grades were never really a big priority to me. In elementary school, my grades generally stayed above a C, but as I grew older they fell, declining in middle school. My parents pushed me to do better, but I did just enough to get by. My mind just didn't take to sitting in a classroom. I see now that I wasn't stupid or immature, but perhaps the contrary. My brain ran on a different level; testing and traditional schooling wasn't what I needed. I wasn't meant for a cookie-cutter curriculum. I excelled in English and creative writing and struggled with science and math. I liked looking slick and impressing girls. I made sure I danced with as many girls as I could at the dances and made out with them outside of the dance—when my mother wasn't chaperoning. My mother worked at the Woodland Park Pregnancy Center for most of my early childhood. Abstinence from sex was the philosophy of her business. She would go into the high school and teach abstinence. One of the strategies used was showing them grotesque pictures of genitalia that had been infected with STDs.

This was very embarrassing for me, being a young man going through puberty. I felt my parents had high and unreasonable standards. I felt like they wanted me to be outcast, so they could control who I would be as I grew up. This mentality, combined with the constant push to be religious, made for a strong need for rebellion inside me. I became angered that my parents would go to such lengths to try to control me. Couldn't they trust me? Or trust that I would turn out ok, even if I made mistakes?

In eighth grade, my first mind-altering substance ingested was Coricidin, cold pills also known as Triple Cs. They were cheap and had a strong effect on me. They were easy to access as well, a condition of my environment. I can remember my first time taking them and the strength of the effects. I took them in the middle of class and the effects lasted into the night. I didn't know it back then, but I was already hooked on changing my reality. My brain chemistry contoured perfectly to the high of the drugs. It nurtured my desire to constantly escape and be someone else. Also, during spring break that year, I smoked weed for the first time. I spent the day stoned and skateboarding, and watching my friend puke in a ditch behind Safeway. The only time you have fun watching your friend puke in a ditch behind Safeway is when you're high on weed.

The high I got from pot was amazing to me. To think that something so simple like smoking a plant could make me feel like it did was fascinating. It helped me escape reality. It gave me a new perspective and relaxed all those thoughts of fitting in or being cool. I felt more like myself than ever and less stressed over who I thought or who my parents thought I should be.

There are no words that can describe what door opens when you choose drugs and feel like you've come to terms with what's been missing your whole life. When you're high, your relationship with a substance can feel like a love story. It's like the drug understands you better than a person ever could. This is how it started for me. Some people aren't sure how they feel about drugs the first time, but I was. I knew deep down this was going to be an asset in my life, whether it resulted in negative consequences or not. Deep down, I knew the danger that the passion for this substance could cause, but I had no concerns about it. The feeling was too strong, and because I felt like I had been sacrificing happiness to hide secrets in my mind, drugs felt like the perfect antidote. This was to be a new road for me . . .

Chapter 2

High School Blues

"When a child first catches adults out—when it first walks into his grave little head that adults do not always have divine intelligence, that their judgments are not always wise, their thinking true, their sentences just—his world falls into panic desolation. The gods are fallen and all safety gone. And there is one sure thing about the fall of gods: they do not fall a little; they crash and shatter or sink deeply into green muck. It is a tedious job to build them up again; they never quite shine. And the child's world is never quite whole again. It is an aching kind of growing."

– **John Steinbeck, East of Eden**

In high school, my mentality started changing, becoming more introverted and quiet in my classes. I also became less confrontational. Being a freshman can be intimidating, and there was less attention from girls to fuel my ego, since they had directed their interests toward upper classmen. I still had fun though. I also discovered I liked using marijuana on a daily basis. Beyond the experimental stage, I would ditch school to go to my friends' houses and smoke all day. I got lost in the pot fog and had too much fun doing it. I started ditching school at least three times a week.

Playing football deterred me from ditching school until the season was over. As soon as the season ended, I increased getting high and decreased school attendance. Around the end of winter of my freshmen year, I had been looking for weed all over the school but hadn't found any. My buddy Eric and I searched the grounds, asking everyone we knew if they had any. Finally, we came across an upper classman who always had weed and connections. He had said he was out of weed but had opium. I had no idea what opium was, but knew a lot of my friends had tried it before.

I was nervous about the buy, but I felt pressured to follow through. I thought if everyone else had tried it, then why shouldn't I? I gave the dealer $15, and he gave me a gram of opium in a small cellophane wrapper. When lunch time came, we snuck in through the back window to my friend's house by the school. I pulled out the cellophane and finally got a good look at the red and purple rock that I had been toying with in my pocket during class. The moment before getting high is a rush in itself, especially if it's something new. I opened it up and loaded it in the pipe. My friend showed me how to smoke it, and then I hit it myself.

It tasted sweet and had a scent similar to potpourri. Then the high hit me. It was a little different from other drugs I had tried and a bit scary. The high was stronger and more relaxing. I broke a new barrier of reality that day. I made it back to class and a few of my older peers could tell I was zoned out on something. They came over and started picking on me and messing with me. They drew on my face and fixed all their jokes and attention on me. I couldn't wait for class to be over. I held back tears because of how intense the teasing felt under the influence. I just wanted to enjoy my high and be left alone.

Eventually, I made it home that day but don't remember much, except for my parents going through my backpack and finding the remainder of my opium. I argued and argued and tried to convince them it was weed, but two purple rocks in cellophane looks painfully nothing like marijuana. The truth came out and my parents panicked. I got the cliché speech on how addicting opium and opiates were and how I was choosing a path of destruction through smoking weed every day and ditching school.

Despite those horrible couple of days of humiliation and unearthing of my addictive behavior, I continued to smoke weed as often as possible. I remember getting headaches and not being able to sleep when I didn't smoke that day. It was a foggy existence, not just because I was high all the time, but because of how I had labeled myself or how I felt I was perceived by others—and I became depressed. I felt that I was being judged by my parents, family, and those from church or society. I believed my parents were concerned about our reputation, which explained their tight rules and their persisting to control me.

This belief was partially true, and it was emotionally paralyzing for someone like me, who had grown up in the church. I remember being grounded a few times and coming home and doing nothing but sleeping after school or playing video games. Eventually, baseball tryouts came along, and I made the team. That was a good change of pace for me and kept me out of my stoner fog. However, I was still smoking just about every day.

At lunch one day, I went off to smoke with my friends. I saw one of them in Spanish class, a girl named Stacey. When I walked in, I saw her with her head lying down on the desk. I sat down and said hi to her. She looked up, and I saw her face was as white as the walls. As class went on, she went to the nurse. When she left, I knew my risk for trouble had increased. A nice girl like that could get talked into snitching in a heartbeat—especially if she's as stoned as we were.

Trouble

Later that period, sure enough. Five minutes before school was out, the assistant principal showed up in the classroom and asked to see me. My stomach dropped and the blood rushed to my head. I knew what was about to happen, but told myself everything was okay and start thinking of lies and excuses to tell.

"Nate, can you come with me?" he asked.

I got up and took my backpack to the office. Not a word was said between us, and as I approached the office I saw one of my friends I had just gotten high with. He looked up out of the corner of his eye and then Officer Walker walked in. Time moved slowly. Thoughts ran rampant through my head. I was trying to picture every question the officer and the principal would ask and what lie I would tell them to stay out of trouble.

Everyone in the school knew this cop; he was notorious for making kids miserable. He sat down and asked me a series of questions that I can't remember. I tried to deny being stoned. Very quickly, my lies broke down.

I can't remember what was said, but I knew then that the officer was more experienced at this than I. Shame and guilt started to set in, and I remember starting to cry and keeping my head down. My parents were called, and soon my mother walked in. I kept my head down.

"His eyes were super red before he started crying there," the officer said, to make sure it was rubbed in nicely.

I could see in his eyes that I was not a person; I was an object that deserved punishing. The reasons why I used weed, and who I was, were of no concern to him. The officer did his job and that's all he knew. He believed in what he was doing, too. He believed in degrading me and doing whatever it took to prove his point. He believed he was "teaching me a lesson."

The shame was heavy on my heart that day. I went home with my mother and awaited my father's arrival. He got home about 4:40 p.m. Already aware of the situation after speaking to my mother, my dad kept a straight face and looked me in the eyes. He was angry, but he had no clue what to say. There was nothing *to* say. He told me we were going to talk to the baseball coaches at 7:00 p.m. to explain what had happened that day.

When 7 p.m. rolled around, I left with my dad for the high school to face the coaching staff. I had felt shame all day, and I was drained. I did my best to be remorseful all day, and now I would do it some more. I walked in after all the other kids had left and faced the three coaches. I told them about what happened and, as expected, I was kicked off the team. I finished my speech and give them a humble apology, as I was coming down off of my afternoon high. The discussion was over, and I walked out with my head down. "Nate," the head coach hollers, "Just so you know, you're done!" I paused and nodded my head, with tears welling in my eyes. *Yep, thanks coach*, I thought to myself.

A Mountaintop Experience

I now realize it started in these situations: I began feeling like it was me against the world. I began to resent society and all the "normal" people in the world—the ones who decided what was best for me. The ones who decided that I was wrong and bad instead of seeing me for who I was. They labeled me with a number and a consequence. And as I grew older, I learned that these people punishing me knew nothing about my life or my addiction. I guess there are parts of society that think if they place fear and shame of using in your head that it will cause you to cease using. At first I thought it would, but as time went on, I learned to just pretend like I was ashamed.

I took a week off from school to take my grounding at home and clear my head. I came back to school and stayed completely clean. I quit ditching school. I started counseling with my church's youth pastor and did community service at the church as well.

One day, I was doing community service for the head pastor, raking leaves in the parking lot. After about an hour, the pastor told me to stop and said we would spend the second half of the time doing service to myself: This became my first time trudging up the Manitou Incline, a mountain hiking trail that gains 2,000 feet in less than one mile. The incline is equipped with inbuilt railroad ties for the hikers to use as steps to assist in the climb and prevent them from slipping downhill. I watched the pastor march up to the top, and I did my best to keep up. I kept my head down and trudged up this steep and dreadful hill. I finally made it to the top and was congratulated by my pastor. He was so strong and in shape. He ran right back down like a champ. I was impressed and inspired. I wanted to be like that. I glanced around at everyone surrounding me on the top of the mountain and saw the dedication, the sweat, and success. The view from there was like something out of a novel. I looked out over the city of Colorado Springs. It made me forget about my problems. I remembered I was a person. I had a heart. I wasn't a number or just another troubled teen. I was an athletic kid who grew up in the church and had two loving parents. I had a pastor who took time out of his day to spend with me. I was valued, and I was loved.

After a few weeks, I was allowed back on the baseball team. It was like a miracle. I felt like myself again. Our team wasn't great, but we had a blast. Our freshmen coach was awesome and worked well with us. I sensed he had no prejudice against me for my struggles. He looked at me for who I was, not for what I had done. My best friends were on the team, and we enjoyed leaving school early for games and playing hard and having fun during practices. Baseball season ended and, shortly after, so did my freshmen year, which ended positively despite my problems with the law. I spent the summer playing another season of summer baseball, skateboarding, and hanging with my friends. When I wasn't skateboarding, I went on hikes right outside my neighborhood with my friend Ryan.

One day, we ventured through the backwoods by our houses, hiking for about an hour, when we came across an opening that sat on top of a small hill. We found a huge man-made hole that looked big enough for a fire pit. We knew exactly what this place was to become. It was to be our camping spot. Our friend Harry came over and we camped out that night. We called it "The Spot," and it became the popular camp spot for me and my friends. We spent the rest of the summer camping out at the spot and skateboarding.

The nights came and went, and it all went by so fast. Some nights blended in and are hard to remember, maybe because of the weed or just because they were uneventful. Others stand out, leaving indelible marks that emboss emotions into the memory, leaving a nostalgic yearning for those nights with those friends. One night, two girls, Sarah Jane and Katie, camped with me and Ryan. It was our first night having girls out at the camp site. Just before the school year ended, Sarah Jane and I had hit it off. She was popular, and I had had a crush on her since the third grade. Blonde hair, pretty eyes, and a beautiful smile. We had our summer fling, and it was over in a few months, like most high school relationships. We remained friends afterwards.

Skateboarding and Football

At the beginning of sophomore year, I smoked pot and drank a few times, but it was not the main focus of my life. My parents told me multiple times that the football season wasn't going to be good for me if I didn't make it to the gym, but I ignored them; I had my own agenda. I loved skateboarding because it was my choice. My whole life to this point my parents had decided what was best for me. I began to fight for my independence, pushed away from team sports, and did what I wanted.

I almost quit football that year, but my parents convinced me to play one more year. I felt free that summer when I hung out at the skate park or skated around town. I loved the warm weather and loved working hard on my skateboard. I came home dirty from hitting the ground so many times and falling off my skateboard, and sometimes came home with blood on my pants and shirt. I felt like a man. Through skateboarding I found a circle of friends who understood me and shared a rebellious and independent attitude as well.

Skateboarding was the best expression of independence I had ever found and was the first time I had dedicated myself to something willingly. There was an art to skateboarding that no one in the community recognized unless they were directly participating. Thought of as just a sport for the bad kids or the antisocial, skateboarding is full of creativity and lets a young person use his imagination to create his own style. Each trick requires careful calculation in timing and depth perception.

Skateboarding also provided me a way to get around town quicker than walking. I liked the fact that it was an *individual* sport, and I could make what I wanted with it. It taught me discipline, as well, as it is not a sport that provides immediate gratification. Sometimes it would take weeks or months to master a trick or finally jump down a huge staircase and land. Skateboarding was all mine, and I could do what I wanted with it.

So at 15 years old, I started my sophomore year of high school and what would be my last year in football. I did like the game, and I played hard. I laid some big hits despite my size and neglecting the gym all summer. In one game, against a team that had a reputation of playing dirty, I went up against a kid who played outside linebacker and receiver. In the middle of the game, I was covering him far from the play to make sure he was covered and wasn't passed to. I had tripped over myself and fallen down. When I tried to get back up he shoved me down. He pushed me two or three times, and the weight of my shoulder pads made me top heavy and easy to push over. We made eye contact, and he looked down at me with a look of superiority as I lay on the ground.

A few seconds of helplessness felt like a lifetime of frustration. I got up and pushed him back once and retaliated with words. As he walked away, I marked his number in my head and waited patiently. Half time passed, and I kept my eye on him. I watched him like a hawk and waited for my moment. He set up as an outside linebacker on the defense, and I was at wide receiver. I knew a specific play designed for me. "Brown right, quick pitch left." The wide receiver was to "crack back" on the outside linebacker. This meant I was out wide on the field and ran in toward the center of the field, where the outside linebacker is blind to me. As soon as the linebacker sees the running back catch the pitch and start heading to the outside, I'm in his face, and he should be knocked down.

My team got the ball and I was on the sidelines about ready to run the play in from the coach to the quarterback. I told the coach, "Brown right quick pitch left, Coach." He thinks for a minute, and I insist again. He looks out the side of his eye and says "Ok, Nate. Let's give it a shot." I set up outside and scoped this bully, like a pirate looking at a treasure. The ball was snapped, and I sprinted toward him. He didn't see me. It was divine. I got about a foot from him, when he turned and saw me. CRACK! I put my shoulder down and laid him flat on his back. He struggled to get back up, and I shoved him down twice. He was unable to get back up under the weight of his shoulder pads. Revenge is a dish best served cold.

I have many memories of dishing out big hits and feeling like a triumphant underdog. I also recall getting hurt and taking hits, too. Because of my lack of discipline in the gym, my body was undertrained at times. I remember the pain from one injury and exactly how it happened. I went up against a much bigger linebacker and blocked him from a running play, and just then saw another player about to run by me. I stuck out my arm, and he plowed right through it like it wasn't even there. SNAP! My arm extended beyond the normal range of motion about 45 degrees past where it should be at the shoulder joint.

I screamed and jogged back to the sidelines in agony. I told the trainer I was hurt, explaining what had happened. He said, "Ok, let's see if you can lift it up." I mustered up all the energy I could and lifted it, ignoring my body's insistence against moving my arm. Inch by inch, centimeter by centimeter, I got it to lift up above my head. "Get back in there!" he says and smacks my butt for a jump start. I spent the rest of the game with my arm hanging limp by my side and doing my best to make contact only on the good side. I could have complained, but it made me feel tough.

A few days later, my arm was x-rayed. I learned there were shattered bone fragments scattered in my joint, and the growth plate had separated. I spent the rest of the season on the sidelines, wearing my sling with pride, like a battle scar, proud to tell the story and sure to mention that I played half of a football game with a broken arm.

The season ended, and I anticipated more free time for skateboarding and hanging with friends. This particular year, I wore a tie and dress shirt every day to school for no reason but to be different and do something no one else was doing. I always maintained an attitude to be different. Not to stand out, but to do what is not normal and flow against everyone else—a subtle way to rebel, I suppose.

Trippin'

On Halloween of my sophomore year, a friend brought a toy gun to school as an accessory for his gangster costume, representing the movie *Reservoir Dogs*. Since football season was over, I had bought an eighth of psilocybin mushrooms earlier that day and had stashed it in my backpack ready to go for the weekend. This was to be my first time trying hallucinogenic mushrooms. My friends and I stood in a circle, and I insisted on playing with my friend's toy gun. I pointed it at my friend and said "Die, motherfucker!" At that exact moment, a teacher named Mr. Jimmy was walking by. It looked bad, and it sounded even worse than it was. This was just a few years after the Columbine shooting, which caused school officials to be vigilant about weapons in school, especially guns.

I was taken to the office, expecting to be reprimanded by the staff. While I waited, my friend came in the office and took the toy gun from me, hoping it would keep me out of trouble. Shortly after he left, a cop walked in—the same cop who had busted me the year before for being high. He looked around and said, "What is this about a kid with a gun?" I knew my punishment was going to be more severe than after-school detention. I told him that the report was about me, that the gun was a toy, and I no longer had it. He asked me to follow him back into the office. Leaving my backpack with the hidden mushrooms underneath the chair, I went into the office, where I was frisked and lectured.

Another policeman arrived, and I was lectured some more. I didn't cry like last year; I was more hardened and believed the whole situation was ridiculous. Then my parents arrived. It was like a replay of last year, only I was sober and more apathetic. The cops went to their cars to discuss a charge for me. I sat in the office for a few hours before they came back. The sun went down, the students and staff had left, and my remorse for my mistake grew more and more distant. My perspective of the school darkened with the sun's descent. This wasn't a place for me to learn anymore. This was a sanctuary of shame. I was watching my dreams shatter like they were on a television screen—like I was watching a bad movie. The police returned: I was cited for unlawful display of a weapon.

Months later, the yearbook came out and there was a picture of two student council members, on Halloween, one dressed as a cowboy, holding a gun to a friend's head. It looked comical and innocent. The principal paid no mind and the young lady in the picture wasn't charged with unlawful display of a weapon. They were on student council and I was not. And she wasn't telling her friend, "Die, motherfucker."

The next day, I tripped on psilocybin mushrooms for the first time. Both my parents were home. I had conversations with both of them that day, and when they weren't around, I peeked out the window and hallucinated. I went back and forth between my room and the living room, tripping out in my own little world. It was a nice break from reality. I had wanted to experiment and had found another outlet.

The System

It took a year in the Teen Court system to get my legal issues dealt with. Our first attempt at Teen Court was miserable. I was prosecuted by an adult attorney, even though the proceedings were supposed to be facilitated by teenagers. My parents objected, prolonging the court process, which planted a seed in my head that I had turned out to be a bad kid—or a lowly criminal.

The new charge that came on Halloween, unlawful display of a weapon, didn't slow down my partying. In fact, I was drinking every weekend, but smoked no weed because I might be subjected to random urine analyses (UAs). Knowing the evidence would be in my urine for 30 days, I was careful to avoid more trouble. I sometimes drank during or before school, too. I skateboarded when I could, and I did my best to go on enjoying my life. The drinking helped me escape the pressure from the system and kept me from feeling like a lowlife. I surrounded myself with others who had been in trouble like me, and we drank together. I developed lifelong bonds with some friends despite the trouble and my parents' warnings about keeping bad company. It felt like a new family.

I felt like my parents couldn't understand. They hadn't been through what I had been through. I doubted my parents had ever seen a bag of mushrooms before.

I had now been suspended every year since sixth grade for fighting, smoking weed, and now playing with a toy gun. My grades began to fall again too, except for creative writing. My record was stacking up and my self-esteem was crumbling under its weight.

Fear and Rebellion

It was at this point in my life that I began to feel lost. Fear gripped me. I didn't know it at the time, but I was being led by my fears. Fear from authority. Fear of my turning out to be something I'm not supposed to be. Fear from what I looked like in the eyes of others. I questioned everything my parents had to tell me, partially from being rebellious and partly because my life was turning out to be different from the image they had had for me. Sports were not the cure-all, as my parents had hoped they would be, and I pushed my parents away when it came to confronting problems. I felt I would never please them. The best way for me to communicate was to talk with my peers, some of whom were just as confused as I was. Our answer was to get drunk and party.

I persevered though. Despite fear, buried feelings, and insecurities, I had some of the best times of my life during this period. I had a strong heart then, as I do now, even though I didn't know it back then. Overall, I was a normal kid who partied a lot and did his best to have fun and have friends. I was experimenting and very in touch with my creativeness through skateboarding and writing. I forged some bonds with people that have lasted through the years and will last for a lifetime. I had problems, but I had a grasp on what was acceptable, despite my somewhat careless actions. These were the years that I wish I could remember more.

Spring break had come of my sophomore year, and I spent three days of that camping and partying in the woods. Drinking and driving was common and accepted. Our actions were precursors for what was to come. One night, we left the campsite to gather firewood in the back of my friend's truck. We filled it up, and my friend and I sat in the truck bed. I was sitting behind a long tree we had taken down. It extended about a foot beyond both sides of the truck. As we were cruising back to the campsite, both sides of this long piece of firewood caught onto two trees on both sides of the truck. The log stayed in place as the truck kept moving forward and I was clotheslined in the chest by the tree. I fell backwards out of the truck onto my back. I laid there and heard my friend yell, "We lost Wilson!"

They stopped and came back to check on me, helping me get the log off me. We got back in the truck and took off after we laughed about it, like nothing bad had happened. We left the log behind. When we got back to the campfire, we realized that if the tailgate would have been up, I would likely have broken my back or neck, and died or been paralyzed.

Other camp nights, I might have spent tripping on logs or falling into hot coals in the fire pit. Drinking, driving, finding where the next party was, talking about who slept with whom and who got a DUI, or who got in trouble for smoking weed was how it went. We built philosophies on rebellion and a punk-rock attitude. We questioned authority and stood by independent thinking. It was freedom at its finest.

Our music and movies were controversial, and I loved the way they made me think outside the box. Movies like *Requiem for a Dream* and *SLC Punk* were some of my favorites. I listened to everything from classic rock and punk rock, and all the way to death metal. Anything mainstream was too cliché for me to have a hand in. Baseball came and went the same as it did last year. The stipulations of my probation were based upon my "Unlawful Display of a Weapon" charge. So I started to smoke pot more frequently again since my probation didn't mandate any UAs. I went to the skate park after school and stayed as long as I could. I had friends who were starting to drive, so I could stay later and get rides home. The end of the school year came, and I was beyond excited for the summer. I had friends who were in the graduating class, and I knew there would be a lot of parties and a lot of fun.

The day after school was out, my buddy Ryan and I were playing pool and getting stoned. We called our friend Lee to see if he wanted to join us. He came over with Sarah Jane and our other friend, Sandi. We got stoned and kicked back. They talked about going to a party that night and how excited they were. Ryan and I stayed behind.

There are times when you look back and wish you had said more or paid more attention to the details in someone's face, or maybe just told them that you loved them and put more compassion behind your goodbyes. If only we knew when our last moments were going to be with the people we lose.

Loss

My mother called the next day to tell me that Sarah Jane had been in a "car-surfing" accident, while my friend Lee was driving. They had been drinking and Sarah Jane and a few other friends had climbed on top of the car while Lee drove around on dirt roads in the woods. Sarah Jane had fallen off and hit her head and was on life support, and was not expected to live.

I called my friends to see if they were okay and to meet up. We got together and decided drinking would be our pain remedy. We were leaving the liquor store and saw Lee at Blockbuster. We pulled in and told him we were sorry about what happened. "You're sorry! Everyone is sorry. Doesn't fucking matter," he said. A part of Lee had given up that day, and he would never be the same. We were all too young and the incident was too drastic to say anything intelligent or inspiring to him— or something to take the edge off of the pain. We left him there at Blockbuster. That was the last time I saw the old Lee.

The funeral was devastating. The church was packed, with everyone wanting to show their respect and condolences. So many young people in tears and a family torn apart. Lee used to have long, dark, and thick hair, almost like a symbol of his free spirit. I stared at the back of his newly shaved head from a few pews back in the church. To me, it seemed to symbolize his free spirit being cut and a sign of his submission to sadness—similar to when Samson had his hair cut in the Bible.

A hole was left in our community with the loss of one young girl. One phrase from a eulogy echoed in my mind: "Don't let her death be in vain." We listened to the eulogies and did our best to expel our emotions and try to get some closure. At the end, we passed her lifeless body in the open casket. I'd been to funerals with an open casket before, but none of them held a pale, beautiful young woman. My best friend, Ryan, stood next to me as he looked at her body and said, "That was the most fucked up thing I've ever seen."

There's an indescribable lack of presence in a dead body that's only understood once you see it. Pale, emotionless, breathless, empty. The concept that their brain is no longer active and their soul is gone is shocking. Their face connects you to your memories of them, but your senses tell you something is wrong and disturbing about the sight of them dead. We made our pass like everyone else, and after the funeral did the only thing we knew how to do when it came to coping with bad emotions—we started drinking. After a few hours, our minds naturally numbed out reality and we laughed again. The laughs were artificial—a temporary fix—but still just that . . . a fix. I realize now that I paved a road when I chose to self-medicate my broken heart. I opened up a highway to self-destruction.

The rest of the summer, my friends and I developed a strong support system with each other. Sometimes it revolved around smoking weed and playing soccer or smoking weed and skateboarding all day. Then we might go out camping and drink the night away. After a few months, we still mourned, but I began to feel somewhat normal again and had good bonds with some great friends. The rest of the summer was memorable, and we made the best of it, despite the recent loss. I think of this time as being the last days I felt normal. I still felt resilient and strong despite the heartaches. I was able to move on and cope. I was still okay with being me. The tension from the funeral was wearing off, and I began to live an average 16-year-old life and started making awesome memories.

New Highs

Just before school started my junior year, I tried cocaine for the first time. I snorted it probably three or four times before the school year started. My first time, I didn't get very high. My friends who had tried it before insisted that I share it with them, and so there was not a lot left for me. A few weeks later I tried it again, and I skyrocketed. I felt great and invincible. A very different high from alcohol, I had even more confidence, something I'd struggled with for years. We skateboarded and drove around town and did lines every hour until a gram was gone between four of us. Later, I went to work washing dishes at a local restaurant called The Swiss Chalet. I was so enthused about the high, I paid no mind to my irrationalities on the drug. I felt cool because of the high and because it just felt good. I used it when it was around, but didn't consider myself an addict.

My junior year had started, and I was loving it. I felt more independent than ever and was living life on my terms. I was partying but kept my grades at a C average, which was good enough for me and better than years past. I did not play football that year. My parents weren't happy about it, but at this point there was no talking me out of it. I felt I couldn't be controlled anymore, and I celebrated that often. The weeks went by, and I thought I had my routine down. My cocaine use started to increase. It started out on the weekends and slowly spilled over into searching for it on the weekdays and even doing lines in the bathroom at school on a few occasions. I recall one time doing a huge line right before gym class and then jogging around the gym and feeling like my heart was going to explode. My life went on like this until homecoming week.

On the day of our annual homecoming bonfire, my friend Tim and I were on the hunt for cocaine at the skate park. Some friends told us they knew our buddy had some, so we gave them the cash and they returned about 30 minutes later. "The guy doesn't have 'blow,' but he has crystal if you want that."

Crystal meth. My friends had all tried it before me, and I had no intention of doing it. I had been warned countless times by friends about why I shouldn't do it. They all said they knew me and knew I would have problems with it. I can recall one night when my buddy Jay lectured me when we were camping and drinking. He had tried it for the first time when he was 11. He was very drunk and was very passionate about how he described the dark side of crystal meth. He described how after you did it the first time you would change. It would change something inside of you and change your heart. Something indescribable, but noticeable and perceptible

My buddy Tim and I thought for a second and, against our better judgement, decided to make the buy. This was the first time trying it for both of us. We waited anxiously for about 30 minutes. The anticipation for drugs is like being in a cage of anxiety. I would create an image in my head of how I would act on the drugs and what we would do throughout the night, daydreams to keep my restlessness at bay. And then along came our sack of crystals.

We sat in Tim's car and weren't sure how to do it at first, so we called our friend. He told us we needed to smoke it somehow, but it had to be on metal or tin foil. We went out to the woods and got crafty and used the bottom of a coke can. We cut the top off and flipped it over. We lit the can and sucked up the smoke through a straw. The taste was bitter; I couldn't tell if it was from the meth or whatever was coming from the aluminum. The can would get hot, and we wouldn't be able to light it long enough to get smoke. We had absolutely no clue what we were doing smoking meth...*or in life.*

We got what we could, and the effect of the drug came strong. I felt euphoric and stimulated with confidence, like my cocaine highs, only stronger and longer. I knew this was a strong stimulant, so to keep from grinding my teeth I found a straw and chewed on that the rest of the night. Whatever was left in the bag we snorted from the tops of our finger tips.

The desire to do more was uncontrollable. We snorted until the bag was gone and then went to the homecoming bonfire. I walked around the fire, chewing on a straw and looking probably more suspicious than I realized. I made rounds mingling with my friends, while avoiding the police patrolling the area. The night was a success in trying a highly addictive and destructive substance. I went home and made it past my parents and then spent the rest of the night on my bed, listening to music and waiting for the sun to rise, so I could go to school.

I went to school still chewing on the straw from the night before. I saw my friend who had got me the new drugs. He took one look at me and the straw and started laughing, as I chewed the straw relentlessly. The effect from the meth had kept me awake, but the high had worn off by the end of my school day. I didn't eat anything the whole day, but didn't feel drained. I was sleep-deprived, but I didn't feel crazy or empty; I just felt like it was a long night of partying.

I went about two weeks without doing meth before I felt the urge to do it again. I knew it was addictive, but had the idea that I could do it in moderation. I hadn't experienced any negative effects yet. However, this night would change all that. I made a connection through a friend at school to get some more. This guy worked at Taco Bell and he looked like a "tweaker." He was the type of person I would never want to be seen with for fear of my reputation. His face was sunken in and his eyes were dark. His teeth were almost destroyed, even though he was only in his late 20s. He talked funny and had an obnoxious laugh. He was the epitome of why you shouldn't do meth—the poster boy for not smoking meth.

We sat at his girlfriend's house, waiting for the meth. Finally, the dealer showed up at the front door. Extra precaution was taken to make sure we didn't see the dealer. "Don't leave the room or else . . ." Tweakers are extra cautious and paranoid. We all stayed put, even though we knew who the guy was. He was the top meth dealer in Woodland Park at the time, and we had all seen him in school and at the skate park. The deal was made, and we separated the meth into two separate sacks: one for me and one for the middle man from Taco Bell.

Then we got high. Their preferred way of using was through a bong, a much more effective way to get a lot more smoke and a much stronger high. They cut a hole in the water bottle, stuck some rubber tubing in the bottom, and then put a meth pipe inside the plastic tube. They also dropped Listerine strips into the water at the bottom, so it would taste minty. They had a hit, and then placed it in my hands. I had no clue what I was doing, so I had them light it for me. I saw the smoke immediately whitewall the water bottle. I started sucking the smoke in and could taste the Listerine and the chemicals from the drug. The smoke was musky, but thin and vapor like, and the taste was artificial. The mint was strong and made it deceivingly pleasant. I sucked and sucked and cleared the bong of all its smoke. I was instructed to exhale it as fast as possible because of how bad it was for my lungs. When I exhaled the smoke, it came out of my mouth thicker than any other thing I had ever smoked. There was so much smoke it looked like it had a life of its own. The huge cloud dispersed through the whole room, and everyone watched with anticipation for their hit.

The effect was immediate and stronger than anything I've ever felt. I looked at the ground for a second, and my perception immediately changed. Everything was amplified times 1,000. This is what Jay had warned me about. The drug crept deeper and deeper into my psyche and took control, leaving me feeling invincible. My body became numb and tingly all the way to my fingertips. Everything was good. Everything felt good. Talking with others felt good. Our ideas were genius. I was full of love.

I can't recall what happened the rest of that night, even though I want to. I want to piece everything together, and I want this fucked up road to make sense. But it's not there. This is a part of what makes recovery so hard. I don't know where to start, and I don't know what I'm missing in those hazy nights. A piece of me is lost in those nights.

After that night, I continued to chase that high every weekend—three or four days out of the week. Signs that I was consistently using were starting to show. My attitude got worse; my grades went down. I lost weight and my eyes were sinking back, along with my cheeks. At least a few times, I was busted at a friend's house for being stoned. On one occasion, I hadn't slept in about two days and then had stopped by the friend's house to smoke weed. "Speeding with the brakes on," we would call it.

Hooked

My parents had come to pick me up. Normally, I would be cautious and spray cologne and make sure I was coherent when talking with them, but at this point my brain was blown. I hopped into the car and they asked me a question. I could hear them talking as we drove forward, but I was stuck in neutral, staring out the window. "Nate! We asked you a question!" My response was slow, overthought, and made no sense. They continued trying to talk to me, but I couldn't respond. I could hear them, but my brain couldn't put it together. I was becoming addicted. All night I would play video games or write in my journal, and then go to school strung out. My soul was darkening.

I still did cocaine and would mix it with meth on occasions. I was always smoking weed, and alcohol was around often too. One Sunday, I did two big lines of cocaine right before church service. My parents were still forcing me to go. I made it about 30 minutes into the church service and remember having the shakes from coming down off of cocaine. I felt like everyone in the sanctuary could see me tremor. At 16 years old, these drugs were taking over my life. I would do meth and be trapped in my room all night alone. My hormones, wild and mixed with meth, were toxic for a young man cemented inside of his bedroom for 12 hours at a time. I spent long nights in a trance looking at *Playboys* and watching late night Cinemax. I would go to school the next day and my privates would be sore. When I walked, my pants would brush against it and hurt, reminding me of my addiction and shame.

I was still serving in the teen court program as a stipulation of my sentence from the unlawful-display-of-weapon charge from the year before. I would go to teen court strung out sometimes and would keep my meth and pipe in my pocket in the middle of courtroom, out of fear of my parents finding it in my room. I would toy with it in my pocket while watching these young offenders get crucified for fighting and smoking pot or drinking. It was tragic to watch them being sentenced and see in them what pain I held inside myself.

I kept quiet and tried to slide under the radar at school and in life. I would party when possible, and my tolerance for alcohol went up after doing so much meth. Prior to my involvement with meth, I used to get sick after drinking a certain amount, but that no longer occurred. I would just drink all night until I passed out. After staying up for two to three days, I would crash in the middle of the night and wouldn't wake up for school. No matter how hard my mom tried, no matter how much she shook me, I was crashed. I think it was around that time that she decided to raid my room and get to the bottom of it. She found a light bulb with a purple straw in my drawer. Since I was new to using meth, I didn't have a proper meth pipe or oil incense burner. Instead, I used a light bulb to smoke meth. I removed the bottom part of the light bulb with pliers and once the bottom was removed, I stuck a spoonful of salt in the light bulb and shook it around. The salt removed the layer of white junk on the inside surface of the glass. Then, I stuck a straw in and I smoked your meth out of the light bulb. I can remember the exact shape of this particular light bulb. The time for intervention had come, and I wasn't anywhere near ready.

Treatment

A friend of my parents owned an outpatient drug therapy business, and they took me there Tuesdays and Thursdays. I took UAs at least two or three times a week. This barely slowed me down. I do recall a few sober days, sitting in the waiting room or in my one-on-one session with my therapist and thinking how gray everything was. There was no excitement in any of this. I did treatment only so I could get through the day without being hassled and make it back to the drugs or doing what I felt like doing.

I had spent two days awake with no sleep with a few friends, smoking meth. I brought the drugs the first night, and after that my friends would buy it through me. I was playing middle man. We invited one more friend over named Patrick. He wanted the drugs we had. We made it look fun. I made it look fun, badass. It looked exactly how I wanted it to. When he asked for his own bag of meth, a light bulb went off in my head. I could use this to my advantage. I could play the middle man better. I could get more drugs out of this. I spent another two days awake, getting high and playing middle man for my friends. I was having a blast. My parents were more trusting of all the friends I was associating with at this time, and who wouldn't be? They were good kids. My buddy and his girlfriend and my girlfriend would all hang out and smoke meth and talk philosophy and doodle and draw for hours on end.

After spending the fourth night awake, we decided to score the last $20 sack of meth on a Sunday before school started the next week. We smoked it. But it was the first time I didn't get high, the first time I had smoked and not felt stimulated or relieved. I just felt empty. All of my faith had been put into that little sack, hoping it would re-spark some personality that had been drained from me from not sleeping and not eating and too much partying the past four days, but no. My friends dropped me off, and I went straight to my room and cried. I was now powerless. I looked in the mirror and saw my sunken dark eyes and that I had lost weight. I would float between 120 and 130 pounds at 5'9" or so. I knew I was an addict that day. I knew I was no longer in control.

Addiction on the horizon

The days and weeks continued, and I could not stop. I managed to pass one or two UAs in three months. I worked my way up the pipeline and got a better drug dealer too. With cheaper drugs and dealing come bigger risks. Every time I went to my new dealer's house, there would be guns and gangsters around. Every time I made a buy or met a new tweaker who was crazier than the last, I became a little more desensitized. I spent time with my dealer and got to know him.

During this time, I dropped out of high school and enrolled in an alternative school in Colorado Springs, but I rarely attended. One day, I was ditching school and getting high with my dealer and some of his friends. I met a guy named Joe who was over there frequently. I recognized him because he wore one of those flat, short-brimmed "ivy" caps. My dealer told me that Joe had ties to the Italian mafia and was from back east.

After everyone had left, and it was just my dealer and me, he explained that Joe had done something bad to the Mexican gang he was associated with. Someone had gotten ripped off. My dealer was housing Joe and giving him safe haven from the Mexicans, but knew someone could eventually find out. After explaining this to me, he handed me a meth pipe and a 9 mm pistol and said, "I've got to get some food. I haven't eaten in days. If you see any Mexicans come through the front door besides me, you have to start shooting. I left a full bowl in the pipe for you."

At 16 years old, with a meth pipe in one hand and a gun in the other hand, I was waiting in my paranoid state for Mexicans to come through the door and start shooting at me. Most 16-year-olds may be gossiping about who is going to prom with whom, or talking up their lives as dramatically as they can to parallel Jersey Shore or Teen Mom. Or some maybe smoke weed and drink on the weekends, and hang out at the skate park or play video games. Not me. I smoked and dealt meth and shook hands with the mafia. People would come over and order guns and bullets and more drugs to fuel their crazy lifestyle. I saw one guy order tear gas grenades and an assault rifle, so he could rob someone and take their drugs and money. And in the midst of the chaos, there I was sitting on the couch, calmly and peacefully smoking my meth. Then I would go pretend to be a normal teenager. I was in over my head.

Each day, I would recollect what I had done over the past few weeks and feel shame. I had no control over what I was doing and was losing touch with who I was. I was supposed to be a good kid. I was supposed to be thinking about college and sports and girls, but there was no way that would happen as long as meth was in my life. I saw the hopelessness in everyone at my drug dealers' houses and the blindness of my friends who were using as we plunged our lives into a downward spiral. The deception of the highs, the good times, and the deep conversations we had when we were high were just wickedness in disguise.

My friend was in philosophy class in a community college program, and we spent days and nights talking about philosophy of life and what we thought was wrong with the world, with complete disregard about what was wrong in our lives. I was sure that the world was twisted and I was driven to do drugs because of that: my parents not understanding, the police enforcement being unreasonable and overbearing in my town and in my life, teachers not caring about me as a person. The truth is, we weren't that far off in our philosophy and perceptions, just tragically driven in the wrong direction to do anything about it.

The time for intervention had come. I made my bi-weekly visit to my therapist's office and sat down. I had just gotten high an hour or two before. Sometimes, I would smoke so much that it made me nauseous, and I wouldn't feel it until I sat down. This was one of those times. I had gotten high at least three times that morning, and the night before I'd spent awake watching porn for hours and practically molesting myself. My raging hormones, mixed with a strong stimulant like meth, made for sexually frustrating nights. I looked horrible, and the chemicals were coming out of my pores and creating a tinted oily layer over my skin.

My therapist looked at me and told me I'd failed another UA. "When was the last time you used?" My instinct was to lie like always, but I was so tired of it. "Today." I squeezed the truth out. In what seemed like disgust, but was actually disappointment, she said, "You're going into detox." My parents were called in. This felt like when they had come to the school to get me when I was arrested over the past two years. The dread is so much worse on meth, and I was so much more defensive because of it, like a hurt animal guarding his wound.

Detox centers were called, but none would take me because I was a minor. My therapist and parents agreed that I needed to be placed in rehab. They agreed to make the necessary phone calls the next day. My parents took my money and my cell phone. I went home and, since I had been up for a day or two, I crashed. I went straight to sleep. Sleep and drugs were the best way to avoid my problems.

Before I had gone to therapy, I owed my dealer $30. Just $30. I got my phone back a few days later and listened to a voicemail he had left. I couldn't understand most of it. but heard severe anger in his tone and the words "MY MONEY!" thrown in too. At the very end, I heard his shotgun cocking in the background. My parents would hardly let me out of the house and I had no idea how I was going to pay this debt. They had taken all my money.

After a few days, I called my dealer back. I suppose he'd cooled down a little bit, because he said he understood and just to get him the money when I could. A day later, I gave him $60 and got high again. Knowing I would be going into rehab soon, I made an intentional effort to do as much meth as I could. My friends that I would get high with looked down on my severe increase in meth use, but we knew we were powerless. The prospective rehab center was booked until mid-July, and it was only May. I still had a couple months to do what I wanted until I went into rehab. I knew my parents couldn't keep me locked up in my room for that long.

IV

My buddy, who was also my other dealer, was a true junkie. He injected meth. He had done it in front of me a few times. I looked up to him and had known him since high school. I aspired to be bad like him. I wanted to be on the streets selling, and doing, the most. Because I knew I would be in rehab very shortly, my mind wandered for ways to get as much meth use in as I possibly could. My friend Patrick and I were toxic for each other and, as badly as we didn't want to drag each other down, the meth would cause us to feed off of each other's addictions.

I can't describe what caused me to do it, what caused me to grab my father's needles out of the closet. I knew he needed them.

It was around this time of my life I remember seeing my father's diabetic episodes. His blood sugar would drop in the middle of the night and he would wake up confused and disoriented, not knowing how to get out of it. He would somehow make his way upstairs through the fog and if he was lucky, before it dropped any lower, he would be able to make a sandwich or get some juice in him. On one occasion, I woke up to him standing in the doorway and staring into my room with the light on behind him. He was breathing heavily, and he didn't say a word for the first few seconds. I raised my head off the pillow.

"I need help, Nate," he said helplessly. It was disturbing. Like he was possessed.. I gathered myself and went and made him a sandwich. He came to very quickly. As the years went on, the diabetic episodes got worse and he would lose control of his temperament and lose control of himself.

I knew injection was the last step toward being a full-on drug addict. I tried it anyway. I grabbed a 10 pack of 1-cc half-inch insulin needles before I left the house that day. We went out and found our drugs. We smoked a little bit and then went back to Patrick's house. It was late. We were listening to the Black Dahlia Murder's song Elder Misanthropy. The singer screamed vile death metal lyrics about being cursed as a vampire. Funny to me that vampires were sort of a metaphor for drug addicts. Always awake at night. Always seeking to quench a never-ending thirst. Maybe God's subtle warning of what was to come.

I guess the rock-bottom feeling of knowing I would go to rehab made me feel that I had nothing to lose: I made a decision with my friend to try injecting meth that night. I thought it would be a last hurrah before I made my way to Glenwood Springs, Colorado, to rehabilitation.

We had no clue how to inject and eventually called my friend and asked him about it. He was furious and said we were stupid for wanting to try. He tried to talk us out of it. I remember the last words he said before we hung up the phone: "It seems like a fun little rollercoaster ride. But once the roller coaster starts, it doesn't stop back at the station." I'll never forget those words, and even though I heard them, I didn't really listen. We injected that night.

I opened up a gate to hell that night. I remember what song I was listening to and what the room looked like. I went to work the next day with my friend and continued on with my life, strung out and plunging through the trenches of being a young addict. I spent the next month and a half injecting when I could and tried to hide it from everybody. I tried to be a "better" tweaker. I learned to eat and sleep better than most, so I wouldn't get lost in psychosis. If I looked like I was holding it together, no one would bother me about getting clean. On the contrary, people might think it's cool or look up to it in a sick way. I would stay up one night and then sleep the next night to stay somewhat leveled.

About a week before I was scheduled to leave for in-patient rehab, I had some money from doing odd jobs with Patrick. I had scored a big sack of meth and was increasing my use, since I knew I would be leaving soon. I poured out lines for everyone. It made me feel like a good person to give everyone a piece of my drug sack. I went to the bathroom to inject. I took the hit, not thinking much of it. All the hits I had done before this were nice little highs that made me light-headed and feel on top of the world. But this hit changed me, much like the first time I hit the meth bong, only 1,000 times stronger.

After I shot up, I felt it hit the back of my throat. It burned. I took a deep breath in. I could taste the chemicals run through the veins in my tongue and the heat rush go to my head. It kept coming fast. It was unstoppable. It felt like I was dying. I thought the bong hits were strong, but they were miniscule and pathetic compared to injection. Something inside has changed. My perception, my chemistry, my hormones. There is no such thing as being impaired on meth. There is only being under the complete control and influence of the drug. I felt the devil thrive and laugh in the midst of my addiction.

After a few minutes, I tried to control my high, catching my breath and latching onto the conversation and engaging myself in it. The conversation was deep, and I felt more passion on an injection high. My brain took on a philosophical view on everything: *I've never felt like myself until now.* I felt as though I'd just filled a void that had been wide open my whole life. My thoughts were clear—crystal clear.

Rehab

I lived like this until the night before rehab. I have no idea whether my parents knew I was using in this time period. I rested that night before, and we left for treatment the next morning. Seventeen years old, IV meth user, and headed to a 6-week treatment center. Depressed, but not suicidal. I still had a big flame inside of me and still had high hopes for the future.

When I arrived at the facility and proceeded through intake, I told the nurse I was a meth addict and an IV user. The owner of the program came in and explained my situation to her. I told her I had used meth.

"Meth is very popular right now. It's a horrible drug and it's exponentially addictive," she said.

She asked how I did it.

"I inject," I stated with no emotion, waiting for a surprised look and negative response.

She paused. She looked at me as if I was already gone.

"You know there is nothing in recovery that will feel as good as when you have injected drugs," she tells me with a look of pity.

I told her I knew that. And I did. But it still hurt to hear. I felt like damaged goods or like I had cancer, and she had just given me a diagnosis of a terminal illness. For some, it can be. I knew there would be work, though, so I moved on.

The next couple weeks were awesome. I felt refreshed. I paid close attention to what my therapists would teach, and I was fascinated by all of it. I learned what happened to my brain and body when I have cravings. Sometimes body temperature would change and heart rate, too. I was taught how to think more rationally. I was beginning to feel like myself again. I was excited for life.

About twice a week the staff would walk us down the street about two blocks to a library, where Narcotics Anonymous meetings would be held. At the end of the meeting on a particular night, I was walking next to my roommate.

He walked with his head down in deep thought and said, "I'm running tonight."

"What?" I asked.

"I'm running away from here," he said. "You want to come with?"

I thought about it for a minute. I didn't want to. But the second I weighed the option to do it, it was planted inside my head that that was the only option. I had this itch for trouble that I couldn't help but scratch. I didn't actually want to do this, but I knew it would be a rush. As an addict in early recovery, my brain needed to feel some type of rush. Sometimes, we would do excessive numbers of somersaults at gymnastics to make ourselves dizzy, or hold our breath and have our roommate push against our chest while we stood up against a wall to pass out. We did anything just for a rush

We had no idea where to go or what to do. But I didn't care. I wanted to be bad. I agreed to it, and we waited until the night staff came in on their shift. About 10 minutes later, when everyone was supposed to be sleeping, we stood by the door. We had our shoes and our clothes on. We looked at each other and prepared each other. We bolted through the door and ran downstairs with the staff yelling and chasing after us. We got outside and ran toward the huge mountain behind the facility. I panted and sucked for air, running for my life up this enormous, steep hill.

I didn't stop to look back, and I didn't give in to any doubting thoughts. If only I put this much effort into trying to be successful and a self-loving person. We made it about a quarter mile before we found a trail and stopped for a break. Too late to look back or have a conscience, we followed the trail down into the town. My roommate was a local to Glenwood Springs, so he led the way. We found lots of friends that he knew. We walked through downtown. I even stopped to talk to the cops that night for casual conversation. My friend scurried quickly as soon as the cops approached us.

"What's up with him?" they asked me.

"I don't know. I just met him," I tried to cover.

We didn't get high, but had a few sips of beer and some cigarettes. In the back of my head, I was waiting to find someone who was in the meth game. That time never came. The night came to a close, and we had nowhere to stay. No one would house us, because we were on the run and a risk for them. At about 4 a.m. we walked to the park. My roommate laid down on a bench and closed his eyes.

"Is this it?" I asked.

"I guess so, bro," he replied.

I looked up the street. I could see the rehab hospital from the park. I told him I couldn't do it, and I walked back to the treatment center.

I rang the doorbell at 4 30 am. The nurse answered the door, smiling.

"We've been waiting for you," she said softly.

What an angel she was to say that. Just a few kind words to welcome me back after what I had been through. No reprimanding or preaching. Just love. She knew what I was going through better than I did. I had never met her, because she always worked the night shift, but she looked and talked like an angel. She looked to be in her mid-50s with short, gray hair and a welcoming smile. She's the reason I knew I had made the right decision that night. The staff took a few minutes the next day to decide whether they would keep me or kick me out. The devious side of me knew they wouldn't kick me out. Deep down, I was a good person with a good heart, but my addict mind would often take advantage of the trust I would earn with my kind personality. I was hardly disruptive and very kind and reasonable to the staff, which was sometimes hard to find in a treatment center full of broken children.

They let me back in. I had the room to myself the next couple days, and I came back to my right state of mind. I realized the reason I chose to do something so foolish was because my impulsive brain was still making decisions for me, a common symptom of meth. I was being run by fear and making rash decisions. What was I scared of? What did I fear? I feared being average. I feared being plain. Maybe part of me just really feared being told what to do by others. My pride stood tall. I didn't want to admit I was wrong. I didn't want to admit that I didn't know what the hell I was doing.

The remaining weeks were great. I stuck to the program and worked on myself. I learned how to have fun sober again. I still made dumb decisions, like sneaking in cigarettes with my new roomie and smoking in the bathroom. I was still young. I made a phone call to my friends, Randy and Patrick, one night when they were getting high. I told them I was set on quitting drugs. I was optimistic and excited for living life.

Randy replied simply, "No you won't. I'll have you sticking needles in your jugular vein. Fuck 'em. Fuck 'em all."

Their voices held a sound of apathy as they spoke to me through the fog of morphine injection. It sounded painfully familiar. It shocked me. I tried to ignore it and stay set on the idea of abstinence from drugs. But their words lingered somewhere in the back of my head.

The rest of my stay in rehab was an awesome experience. I went spelunking, played kickball, learned the basics of break dancing. New things presented themselves all the time. New things to do for sober fun, things I never would have thought of before. I learned a lot about addiction. I continued to learn about rational thinking and problem solving—and about being driven by my emotions. I came to discover that the reason I used drugs was to cover emotions.

I still went to school because that was required. School wasn't a chore though. We learned about interesting things in history. Things that weren't boring. Things that spoke to me through my fog. I learned about the theory that the Teamsters Union ordered the assassination of Robert Kennedy. I was totally captivated by this documentary, and I felt intelligent because I could pay attention during the film. We did work too, though. I opened up about things, eventually. I still held my reputation as "Mr. Excitement" and often kept quiet and introverted.

One of my therapists, Karen, said she knew the first time I showed expression or any of my personality. It happened when she told us we were starting group therapy, and I fell to my knees and cried "Nooooooooo," in an exaggerated joking manner. I cried out to the sky like I was playing the William Wallace role in the movie *Braveheart*, when he screamed "Freeeeedommm!!!!!!" She burst with laughter as I entertained the group. She noted that was the first day she actually saw who I was. I started loving myself that day, something I hadn't done since I had become addicted to meth.

The psychiatrist came in to analyze everyone once a month, and my turn had come to talk with him. I wasn't sure what to expect and didn't think much of it. I was told my drug of choice and the manner in which I used it (intravenously) was very dangerous. They wanted to understand why a kid like me went so hard into the drugs and the lifestyle. Coming from a loving home, with two highly functional parents, why did I turn out this way? I knew other kids who got suspended from school or smoked weed, and they didn't go the route I did. They partied on the weekends and still took care of school during the week or continued to play sports.

Then the psychiatrist asked the gut-wrenching question, "Did something happen in your childhood?" Everything stopped. All my thoughts went blank. My body tensed up and I became uncomfortable. But I didn't want him to know. I acted casual, like I was thinking.

"Hmmmm... Not that I can think of."—the cliché liar's response.

You fuckin' liar.

He sat in silence like he was waiting for me to finish a response. It was almost like he knew something was wrong. Maybe I unknowingly gave off some sign. I did something damaging in that moment: I stuck with my lie.

"No, I can't think of anything right now," I declared. Not far from the truth actually. I had actually come to believe my lie. I'd spent the 10 years believing nothing had happened. I didn't know how to address it or if it was safe to bring it to light.

I had more discussion with the psychiatrist, and I led him right where I wanted him to go. I hinted to him that I was depressed underneath my surface. I told him about how Sarah Jane's death had affected me and some other things too. I hinted there was something going on beneath the surface, but refused to be honest. My addict-self knew it needed this secret to latch to. In the end, he determined I had an underlying depression that was not being dealt with. He was very right.

Released and Relapsed

The day came for my release. I was ecstatic! I showed my excitement and expressed how I felt, and my mother and father soaked it up as well. We made the long, 4-hour drive back to Woodland Park from Glenwood Springs. I don't know if I said much. I was too excited about getting my music back and listening to my "As I Lay Dying" CD. I looked out the window anxiously until it wore me into a nap. No stress, no guilt, no worries. Just freedom.

We made it home, and I got my phone back and my $160 that my parents had taken the day they sent me to rehab. My best friend, Ryan, came over and I greeted him with a huge hug and an overload of energy. He was blown back and overwhelmed. He had that drained look about him. He didn't share the excitement I did. He hadn't had 6 weeks off of drugs. He told me he had used up until the day before and had been up for a few days. I felt bad for a moment, but I was too happy to let it bother me. We drove down to Guitar Center in Colorado Springs, and I bought some things for my drum set, so I could play music for a great sober activity.

I remember how happy I was to be out and to be free. On the 30-minute drive to the city, I put my hat sideways and screamed out the window to people on the sidewalk. I acted like a lunatic. I think I woke Ryan up out of his drug induced fog and might have sparked some inspiration in him. I was hoping so anyway.

On the way back home, we stopped at the skate park. Our friend, Zach, was there. He spelled his name "XAQ" in school and it had stuck with him. The sun was going down, and the skate park was becoming empty. Xaq and Ryan were talking about smoking a bowl of weed. Ryan asked me if I minded, and I said no. I had the idea in rehab that I would not do crystal meth, but would smoke weed and drink. And on my first night out, I fulfilled that reality.

"You sure you want to smoke, Nate Dog?" Xaq asked, knowing I was fresh out of rehab. "Fucking up your life ain't all it's cracked up to be," he said boldly. The way he said that so casually made me believe it. Smoking weed was low on the scale of bad things I had done, so I decided to smoke anyway within the first 24 hours of being out of rehab.

We loaded up in the car and drove around town and smoked a joint. The high was overbearing. I hadn't smoked in so long that the effects hit me like a freight train. My excitement crashed. I couldn't talk, and I was tense and felt guilty about what I was doing. My perception changed: The struggle to be happy was still very tangible around this town.

I remember the conversation they were having was about suicide. Xaq talked about options of how to kill himself. This was a casual conversation. Ryan and I told him he had us, and had enough to live for in our friendship. He stopped for a second and said "Well, fuck you guys! I have a niece to stick around for!" I thought that was hilarious in its own peculiar way. My paranoia dissipated, and I tried to enjoy the rest of the night out.

The mentality of this town, Woodland Park, was dark. It was like a slap in the face the first night out. I was high on a cloud of being free, only to see all of my friends still wrapped in their chains in my hometown. A few nights later, when the weekend came, the rest of my friends got together, and we headed out to the camping spot to get drunk and to celebrate my checking out of rehab. We drank Southern Comfort, and I listened to everyone's stories about what they did while I was in rehab, which was sell and do more drugs. Mainly cocaine. My buddy Gary put his arm around me and told me he'd decided to quit selling because he knew I was getting out soon.

I told them stories about rehab and how I ran away for a night. I told them about sneaking in cigarettes, and they told me about their crazy month of drug dealing. The rest of the night flew by, and I can't remember much else. I do remember the hangover, though. It hurt like hell, and I spent the next day throwing up and healing. More days flew by. I spent some time at the skate park and met with my friend who I had used with right before rehab, Patrick. We went back to his car, and he lifted up the center console revealing a stash of about 20 dirty needles. I looked up at him, and he was smiling. I went back to skateboarding and spent the rest of the day pissed off.

About 2 weeks went by, and I started mixing with my using friends. Patrick had come and picked me up from the skate park with our other buddy, Randy, who was our dealer before I went to rehab. I got in the car and heard, "What's up, ya chubby motherfucker?"—a compliment to the healthy weight I'd put on in rehab.

I was glad to see him, though he was obviously strung out. We spent the night looking for something for them to smoke meth out of since they had no needles and no pipes. I thought I could manage this. I thought I could be the only one who didn't use even though everyone around me was high. There's a saying I learned in rehab, "If you go to the barbershop, you eventually get a haircut." I was in total denial, and on that particular night, I didn't use. But three days later I did use. And I shot it up. It was like the first time all over again. I had control over the high and felt like I was right where I belonged again. The high was smooth, and I felt more mature, like I was mature enough to handle the drug this time.

My life spiraled out of control quickly. I went back to searching for it every day. I quit going to my outpatient therapy and quit taking UAs. I made a connection with my old drug dealer. The game was deeper and the connections to drugs were stronger. I had been attending alternative school when I felt like it, but my addiction had now taken control of me again.

I took a road trip to La Junta, Colorado, to see family and showed up strung out. The paranoia was ruling my mind, and I thought my whole family was talking about me when they weren't. I told my mom, and I sounded insane. I caused a small scene and left abruptly to go sleep in my parents' van. For a few hours, I tossed and turned and screamed to myself. I set the car alarm off while everyone was asleep from violently thrashing around in the van. My life went on for a few more months like this, and my parents eventually kicked me out of their home on New Year's Day 2006, when they found a receipt for syringes on my bedroom floor.

New Year, New Me?

New Year's Day, 2006, I left my parent's house after doing a shot of cocaine. I had spent the New Year's Eve drinking and snorting cocaine. After everyone fell asleep, I started shooting it up. I was totally numb from the drugs during this time in my life, and my attitude in general was insensitive. I wanted drugs and nothing more. I withdrew, isolating myself socially. The only reason I tolerated being around anyone was so that I could get something from them. Drugs, money, a ride, or a place to stay. I was toxic, with a nice personality to disguise it. Others thought of me as friendly and easy to get along with, which wasn't completely false, but my motives were self-serving. When I got kicked out, I stayed with some friends in Manitou Springs. Marijuana was their drug of choice, but I brought meth around enough to where they would use it often. I brought sketchy people over and would sell drugs out of the apartment with little hassle. It was a party house and, for them, it was probably more fun and exciting than bad.

A group of girls who went to Manitou Springs High School came over, and one had caught my eye. Her name was Shannah. My roommate arranged a meeting, and we decided to hang out a couple days later. We'd had no previous conversations except for hi and bye. She told me her dad was a meth addict and about the hard times she had gone through when he went to prison. We hung out often, and eventually she became my girlfriend.

Later my roommate told me she was pregnant. I was stopped in my tracks for a moment, but she later explained the baby wasn't mine and that she had been pregnant for a few months. She said I had nothing to worry about, that her dad would take care of the baby. I argued back saying that I—and my junkie lifestyle—had no business being around a baby. I persisted, and I broke off the relationship with her.

I kept doing my thing. Drugs, weed, some drinking. Everything was gray, and I had no direction. For some reason, I still felt like I was accomplishing something every day. I was on the hunt for drugs daily. It was like I was making a statement against society. Leaving my mark. Living in the struggle or the hustle. I was broken. The system was broken, so I lived outside of it. I lived in the underworld of drugs and misfits to prove that I didn't have to do what they told me.

A couple weeks later I reconnected with Shannah. She convinced me we belonged together. We got back together. She insisted I meet her dad. I had heard the stories of him from my roommates. He had done 10 years in prison in Texas. When I walked into his bedroom to meet him for the first time, he said, "You're the boy that made my daughter cry."

I froze. He was smaller than I expected, but I had heard the stories about him. He had a few ounces of weed, and we came over to help him weigh it into sellable quantities. He told me more about how he had been to prison, and, eventually, I opened up the topic of meth. We talked about how much he paid for his drugs versus how much I paid and how we liked to use it. He injected too. We smoked a lot of weed that night, and I went home with a new connection and friend to use with. A few days later, we hung out and shot meth together. I would get high with her dad and do my best to be her boyfriend. Her dad liked me because I was a nice guy. I was addicted, but not a snake out to hurt his daughter. She was 14 years old at the time and smoked almost as many cigarettes as I did, even though she was pregnant.

Youngest Tragedy

I got a phone call one night from her dad, saying Shannah was in the ER. He said he had been with her all day and left only a few hours to go to work, and in that time she'd had her baby in the apartment. He came and picked me up, and we stopped at the apartment before seeing her. I walked in and saw a small dried-up puddle of blood soaked into the carpet. I pictured what my girlfriend had gone through and what the premature baby would have looked like. I pictured blood, and I visualized her crying and in pain. I pictured a premature baby that could hardly make any noise, struggling to cry.

"We need to clean this up, so she doesn't see this when she gets home," he said.

But first, we got high. He loaded up a mound of crystal shards into the spoon and dissolved it. I watched the dark ritual of him sucking up the murky and thick water back into the syringe. This hit was big. I was higher than a kite and all my stresses were relieved, and so were his. I cleaned up the carpet. I remember how dark it felt. Like darkness lingered in the apartment. The drugs helped me block the darkness out.

About an hour later, we made it to the hospital and I sat next to her on the bed. She smiled when she saw me, and I couldn't understand why, after all the pain she had just gone through. I was still flying high from my shot of meth and felt awkward and tense with her family around. I had no words for her. Nothing that would have made sense or helped her in any way. I was just there, and I guess for her that might have been enough.

The next few days her mother stayed with us at her dad's house. We kept our meth use in low frequency and kept it under the radar when we did use. Time went by and the pain seemed to have found its way to the back of her mind, so she could try to be young again. Her dad and I started using more, and I started turning into an unavailable boyfriend. I was more concerned with getting high and selling drugs. I was constantly trying to act normal around her friends and act like nothing was wrong, even though I was strung out. I was always silent and awkward. I wasn't a party animal; I was a tweaker. We had broken up and got back together a few times, and this was now the routine for us.

Junkie

Around this time, I became especially close with my friend Xaq. We had both just turned 18. We had been hanging out and using together steadily since I had gotten out of rehab a few months earlier. Both of us struggled with depression and did our best to support each other, but we were toxic for each other. Shannah had cheated on me when I was on a particularly bad meth binge, and I didn't take it well. I recall being in a particularly bad argument with my parents that day. I lied to them. I told them I had been molested by an older male next door when I was a child. This lie haunted me for years to come. I couldn't tell them the truth about what had actually transpired between the babysitter and me, because in my conscious mind I actually didn't know that had happened. After three days without sleep, finding out she had cheated, and after the lie I told, I took an X-Acto knife and carved the word "Junkie" into my arm. I carved with self-hatred and contempt against myself while lying on my bed. The scab stayed on my arm for about two weeks. The day after I did it, while I was getting high with Xaq, I rolled up my sleeves and he saw what I had done.

"Jesus, Nate Dawg! I didn't know it was this bad for you," he consoled.

We constantly spoke about getting clean and bettering ourselves. And we would manage to stay clean for a few days or maybe even a week or two, but continued to fall off the sobriety wagon. After this day, we made a plan to clean up, and we gave it our best effort. Our times when we were off meth were fun. We drank together, skated, double-dated.

We sometimes experimented with other drugs. We injected psilocybin mushrooms at one point. Xaq endeavored to come up with ideas to stay clean and have healthier fun, but deep down I knew all I wanted was more meth. Xaq would open up conversation and pour out his heart to me sometimes, but I had nothing to offer.

We'd had about a week and a half off of meth and one night we were smoking weed, driving around looking for something to do. We decided to go to Denny's restaurant, but couldn't remember where in the Springs it was. I called my buddy Randy, who knows the streets well. He told me where Denny's was, but added that he had something for me since he still owed me money. I knew exactly what he was talking about. My meth had finally come through. I had given him money about two weeks prior and never got anything for it. We met up, and he reimbursed me with well over what I had paid. Xaq and I sat in a dark parking lot and loaded up our needles with some of the purest meth I had seen in weeks. I was tense and anxiously anticipating my high to flood my brain. The high was always so intense after not using for a couple weeks. I looked over and saw a sadness in Xaq as he loaded up his shot. Like he didn't want to be getting high. I ignored what I saw and got ready to shoot.

"One of us is going to be dead before we are 21 years old, Nate dog," Xaq said.

I paused for a moment and thought about what to say. I could have said he was right, but I ignored him and went about my shot. I could have said he was right, but I stayed ignorant. I could have said he was wrong and inspired him to keep pushing through the bullshit. I could have said he was wrong and we were just having fun. I could have lied. There was no telling what was going to happen. We got high and ignored the truth.

After a few days of binging and becoming miserable again, we decided to try to get clean again. We thought maybe a change of scenery was what we needed. We went to Summit County and stayed with some friends. Our idea of getting clean was using anything that *wasn't* meth. So instead of injecting meth and smoking low-quality brick weed, we snorted cocaine, drank beer, and smoked the best marijuana in the state. This was my compromise with my addiction at the time.

Everyone else had a blast, and I can recall a few nights where I let loose and opened up a bit after a few too many beers, but for the most part I was miserable. I was crashing so hard, and even though I'd said I wanted to be clean, I had no intention of doing so. I didn't talk to anybody. I purposefully built walls and shut everyone out. After a few days, my patience gave way, and I caught a ride back to Colorado Springs. This was the first time I can remember Xaq being mad at me. He told me he was going to stay back because he wanted to stay clean, and he thought he could stay off of meth up there in Summit County. We parted ways, and I headed back to the Springs. Inevitably, I got high with my ex-girlfriend's father when I returned.

Shannah's father, Ray, had a girlfriend who wasn't an addict and was for the most part normal. She was a "normie." She said she found some temporary work for me at her office. She wanted to see me do well. They wanted to try me out for three days and see if I could hack it. Ray had given me a line that morning before we headed out for work on the third day, almost like a reward for working. I snorted it in the bathroom. It reminded me of high school, except I was better at it now. I worked for 12 hours and went home. They said it would take a week to get my check. Not ideal for an addict, but I had no choice but to wait.

XAQ

I had heard Xaq was back in town, so I called him and went over to his house when his parents were gone. I walked up to his house and saw him and another buddy smoking outside. I guess he had been back in town for days, and I had no idea. His pupils were big, and I could tell he had been up for days.

There's a specific look I see in meth users that has always disturbed me. I've seen it in my best of friends—pupils so big their eyes are consumed by black, oily skin with chemicals leaking out of their pores, and an animated and often smiling face that looks like the mind that lies behind it has no control, or doesn't even belong to this person in this body. When those dark eyes look at you it's like they're not seeing you. You can tell they're hallucinating and taking you in, like they are possessed and someone else is looking at you.

Our buddy, Kevin, was over, too, and we were all drinking that night. Xaq's girlfriend was downstairs and apparently distraught from Xaq's wild, schizophrenic behavior. I went inside and saw her try to leave, and Xaq grabbed her by the arm and tried to pull her back. Kevin and I told him to let her go. This is the first time I had been mad at Xaq. His addiction was consuming him, and he was acting like a maniac.

The rest of the night we drank, and Xaq talked about killing himself, which wasn't unusual. He had been talking about it for years now. Kevin told me to stay here and make sure he didn't do anything stupid and I agreed. We hung out for a few more hours, and, eventually, I passed out from drinking. I woke up and saw Xaq sitting next to me. He had his hands over his stomach. He didn't look over, but he knew I was awake.

"My liver hurts," he said slowly. "I think it's from the whole bottle of aspirin I just took," he said.

He stared blankly at the wall. The house was silent and empty. I sat up and tried to shake my hangover and get out of the fog.

"Xaq, you have to take care of yourself bro," I said to him with an annoyed tone.

I talked to him like his attempt at suicide was vain and obviously mistaken. I was angry that he didn't have more stamina or tolerance for this lifestyle. I told him I had to leave for school and left very quickly that day.

A few days later, the time came for me to pick up my check from working with Ray's girlfriend. I was hanging out with friends and had my dealer lined up for when I got my money. My friends were waiting back at the apartment for me to come back with drugs. I drove by myself to get my check. I showed up to work and Ray's girlfriend handed it to me in person. She knew my addiction and knew me. She gave me a quick 5-minute lecture on spending my money on something other than drugs. I shook my head and looked her in the eye and smiled.

On the drive back to my friend's house, my friend Tim called. He stated very bluntly, "Xaq hanged himself last night." I paused for a second and snapped my cell phone shut. I called my dealer and told him I was coming over, and I didn't answer a phone call from anyone for the rest of the night.

Chapter 3

Becoming a Young Man . . . and a Bigger Addict

"I don't want to be a man," said Jace. "I want to be an angst-ridden teenager who can't confront his own inner demons and takes it out verbally on other people instead."
"Well," said Luke, "you're doing a fantastic job."

Cassandra Clare, City of Ashes

After hearing about Xaq's death, I wanted nothing to do with anybody. If I talked to anyone, all it would do is slow down my pathway to drugs, or I might have to share my drugs. Or I would have to sympathize with others who were hurting as bad as I was. Even worse, I would have to confront my own feelings and emotions.

I had no desire to use my empathy to help others or help myself. The second I snapped the phone shut I made a decision to be all about me. I didn't want to be bothered with conversation; I didn't want any exchange of feelings either. I was defined by narcissism and fear. I was fearful of what people might think of me and how shitty of a friend I must have been. If I opened up and told them about how bad I knew he was hurting, I would be to blame. After all, I knew he was suicidal, and he was my best friend. We fed off each other's negativity, and I felt I had fueled his addiction and sadness. I had no answers, and nothing to offer anyone anyway. My mind was set on drugs, so I made my way to the dealer's house.

I showed up with money in hand and anxiously awaited. I tried not to tell anyone my best friend committed suicide. I gave way eventually, though, and I told a few people in the house about what had happened.

"Damn, that's crazy bro," and a couple other cliché responses were all I got out of anyone.

I didn't care. I yearned for someone to see my hurt deep down. But I wanted my meth.

I waited for two long hours for my dealer to get back with the drugs. Two excruciating hours of me stuffing my feelings and ignoring the truth. My phone was blowing up from people asking if I was okay. My family and my friends. I ignored it all. I wanted my meth.

Finally, they came. I paid for a "teener", which was 1.75 grams. and wasn't sure what I was going to do with all of it. I did my first shot at my dealer's house. That wasn't enough. I spent the night driving from Colorado Springs to Woodland Park and driving on back roads through the forest. I would stop to shoot up every 30 minutes to an hour. I probably shot up 10 or 12 times over the course of 10 hours and didn't feel like I got high once. My mind was somewhere else and not in the moment. I was running. I was running from ghosts. I drove through the back woods for no reason. I thought I was searching for something, but I was running from my family and friends. Running from help and running from confronting my pain.

I drove around the county going through more back woods. I was driving on a trail through national forest when I came up on a narrow trail with cops driving the opposite way. They pulled over and waited for me to get closer. The cop rolled down his window and signaled for me to talk to him. I wasn't scared or paranoid. I didn't care about anything.

"Have you seen a blue truck around here?" he asked.

"Sure haven't," I replied.

"Kids causing trouble," he said.

"I'll keep a look out," I said.

"Stay safe," he looked away and waved.

I drove on for about ten more minutes and shot up again. My parents and friends were looking for me but had no idea where I was and I didn't care. I made it about me, and I was wrong for it. The consequences were waiting right around the corner.

The drugs ran out, and I made it back to my friend's house, where everyone had gone to drink the pain away that night. Everyone was asleep except for a few. It was about 4 or 5 a.m. I liked it better this way. Large crowds intimidated me when I was high—or all the time, since I was always high. A few close friends came out to talk to me and make sure I was okay. I spent the rest of the morning making my rounds and calling friends to tell them I was okay. I made calls to check on others and to make amends for being selfish the night before. Guilt and fear were strong in the back of my mind. Guilt from not helping Xaq before he killed himself. Guilt from not being there for friends. Guilt for being a junkie. My guilt had no end, and it fueled my cravings for more drugs.

The long-awaited hit

I had shot up about 10 to 12 times throughout the night and didn't get high once. I felt myself under the influence, but never got the rush I wanted. Too much dope on the mind. Later in the day, after seeing friends and family, I made my way back to Randy's house. I hadn't cried yet. I was too numb. I finally gave way, as I sat on the floor in his room. In the middle of my bawling he looked down at me.

"You want drugs?" he asked.

I didn't look him in the eye; I just nodded my head yes. He loaded up a big shot for me. I felt like I was dying again. I remember the exact vein I hit and how it instantly ceased the pain. I finally got high. One shot. Not 20 shots but, finally, just one shot. This is what addiction was. Going through days of hell and shot after shot just to get this one high.

I made my way back to my friend's apartment and rested for two days until the funeral. I wanted to be somewhat clean when I attended. The funeral was dark. That church was the most hopeless room I had ever been in. The service was held in the same church as Sarah Jane's funeral two years prior. As I entered the church, I kept my head down and rushed in before most people were there. I looked up at the projector screen and saw pictures of Xaq and cried before any of my friends would come in and see me. More people were pouring in, so I wiped my face dry and walked back a few pews and sat down by a friend. People would hug me from behind and I had no idea who they were. I just kept my head down. I finally lifted my head to look at the pastor. His words were empty to me. I felt like no one really knew the real Xaq.

"I know some of us are a little numb from this tragedy," the pastor said.

He looked me right in the eye when he said this. The pastor knew me personally from church. I had been clean only a couple days and couldn't tell if he was talking to me or if I was being paranoid. The rest of the funeral was painful and hollow. The pastor called Xaq by his little brother's name multiple times while reading the eulogy. The funeral was a disaster and our tears were now vain.

"His name is Xaq!!!" his sister cried out his name and left the room and didn't return for the rest of the service. It was a catastrophe. It was tragic enough on its own and now the funeral was ruined.

The days following were filled with ignorance of truth and excessive drug use. Anything I could do to hide from myself. In days past, even though I was on meth, I slept, ate, and gave the perception I was functional. But after Xaq, I quit caring. I made an intentional effort to not sleep and not eat. I wanted to look like hell, and I wanted to be as dysfunctional as possible. This was my cry for help.

I crashed after spending days awake. This was the type of sleep my mother couldn't wake me out of a few years back. There have been times I've had people shake me or slap me a little bit, and I still wouldn't wake up after a crash like this. But this time, only a few words were spoken, and they raised me from the dead.

"Morgan died," my friend Tim stood above me and told me.

I sat straight up in shock. I wasn't sure whether he was serious or not.

"Who told you?" I asked.

This couldn't be real. My best friend died ten days ago, and now a girl I had known since 4th grade—the girlfriend of one of my best friends—had died in a drinking-and-driving accident? I came to, out of my hazy state, unrecovered from my last binge. With no emotion he confirmed it was true. I wanted to cry, but I didn't. I didn't even try. I hadn't even mourned for Xaq yet.

Self-Destruction

This is when things went out of control. No sleep, no food. Money was running out, and my dealing can't support my habit anymore, so I began robbing and stealing. I saw the news for a brief moment warning the public to lock their cars if they were around Garden of the Gods park; that was because of me and my crew. Every day moved so fast and so much trauma happened that my brain couldn't keep up. I didn't talk anymore; I just waited for the next high—barely communicating with others; only enough communication to get me high.

The voices in my head were getting louder and starting to drown out everyone else's conversation. Everyone smiles around me, even if it's not much, but I don't smile at all. I have no emotion, and I am nothing. I am nothing but a drug addict. That's it. As soon as I drop a hit in my veins I'm ready for the next. It's all I think about. I can't control myself or act like I'm okay anymore.

Weeks went by. Ryan and I sat on his front porch one hot summer day. We were waiting for some friends to get back from the liquor store. I had been up, but hadn't been high in a while.

"Nate, you've been getting pretty high every day, man. I'm worried about you. You've been going too hard, man," he said. "Why you gotta act like this?"

I sat for a second and thought. I didn't have a good answer. I didn't know why. I was being selfish. I sat for a few seconds longer and declared, "I'm slowly killing myself."

Honestly, I didn't want to kill myself. I wanted some sort of attention I wasn't getting before. Maybe some type of attention I didn't get in childhood? Maybe too much attention in childhood? After I spoke those words, though, I manifested that reality. I changed when I said that. My addiction and demon heard me say that and began to take control. I lost another chunk of my heart when I spoke those suicidal words.

From then on, every shot I put into a spoon had more crystal shards than the last. At this point, I was doing my best to commit suicide. It never seemed to work. I learned that meth is just so hard to overdose on. I ended up hurting my brain and my mind. I distanced myself from anyone and everyone, and that was the loneliest I've ever been.

My reasoning for using drugs had changed. At this point, I barely got high anymore. This isn't fun now. I wasn't doing this to be cool anymore; I was doing it because I knew no other way.

After a day of driving around with others like me, we made our way back to the tweaker pad. The day was going by fast, and everything seemed to calm down for a few minutes. My buddy mixed up a meth shot for me in another room. I sat in silence and he brought me the needle. I took the hit. I felt the drug kick in and felt it run from my vein to my heart, then felt the chemicals and heat rush to my head. *I feel normal. Finally, after chasing this high for a week or two, I feel like myself.*

My buddy, Ducks, was on the other couch. He watched me get high, and I could see a look of pity and confusion on his face as I finally started talking for the first time in a while. I opened up because I could feel again. I felt like meth was a part of who I was. We talked about Xaq, about this life we're living. We talked about how broken we were. Ducks started to cry as he talked about missing his parents. We were both on the same level. I started to tear up too. We talked about how neither of us had talked to our families in weeks or months, and they had no idea if we were dead or in jail.

This talk was almost therapeutic for me, but there was still no solution between us, only sadness and a perpetuation of more sadness. My high wore off about 15 minutes after my shot. The voices in my head started talking again, and I felt like everything was going faster around me. The stress made me tense, and I was back to not being able to communicate, back into my bubble. Like clockwork, the drugs ran out and we went back out onto the streets to look for things or people to rob.

ATF

I don't remember much in this 2-week window, but I do remember lending Randy my car to score drugs while we waited at his house. I tossed him the keys, and we paused and stared at each other.

"Is everything okay?" he asked.

"Yeah, I think so," I replied with skepticism, not sure if this uneasy feeling is from paranoia or instinct.

About 10 minutes after Randy left, my friend and I were bored and searching the carpets for meth and talking randomly about nothing.

KNOCK KNOCK!

"Who's there?!?!" I asked.

"Mike Grace!"

It must be one of my buddy's customers.

I opened the door.

CRACK! The door got kicked into my face, and I threw my cigarette behind me in shock.

"ATF!!! Hands in the fucking air!!"

In that split second, my stomach dropped and my adrenaline kicked in. There was a gun directly in my face. I knew I was in trouble. I'd had a warrant out for only one day. The lead cop took me to the back.

On our way, I asked, "You guys have a search warrant or what?"

I felt the cop's grip on my arm tighten, and he started pushing me faster into the room. I try to hold back as we near the wall, but I see he has no intentions of slowing to sit me down and talk.

SLAM!!! My head and body go into the wall.

"I don't give a fuck about a search warrant, boy! Get on your knees!"

He peeled me off the wall and forced me onto the floor in a kneeling position. I peered up with a look of defiance on my face.

"Where's Randy?" he demands.

"Who's Randy?" I tried not to smirk.

He gets in my face and asks, "You been shooting speed balls with him?"

"I only shoot meth, sir," I replied.

He stopped and waited for his backup to search the house They asked me a few more questions, but knew I would continue to play dumb. They gave up and took me out to the car and had the local police take me for booking. I had never been to jail before and had no idea what to expect. Of course, the worst-case scenarios ran through my panicky head. Getting raped, beaten; I'm sure everyone in there wants to beat up a skinny tweaker like me for no reason.

The ride to the jail is long and quiet. I have nothing to say, so I just feel hatred. I hate the cops in the front seat. I wish they had a life like mine. I wish they felt my pain. I'm still strung out, and for a minute I start to believe I can telepathically communicate my pain to them. My psychotic meth trances were becoming stronger. When I could see the jail from the car window, I snapped out of it and came back to reality.

Fear ran deep behind my eyes, but I didn't show it. I could see an inmate mopping the floor from the window in this room. He was wearing a green jumpsuit. A cop walked through the door and handed me a paper. He said all I had to do was sign this paper and I'm released. I couldn't believe it. I was given a paper for another court date and then taken to the downtown precinct. I would say I got off lucky, but I was probably better off in jail.

At the same time that the ATF were raiding Randy's house and arresting me, the cops tried to pull Randy over in my car. He ended up in a high-speed pursuit chase and outran the cops in my Chevy Blazer. He ditched it on the side of the road and ran on foot after he lost them on the road. The cops eventually found my Chevy on the side of the road and impounded it.

Groundhog Day

I should have taken this night as a hint. I should have called my mom and told her to send me to rehab. I walked about 2 miles to my hotel room and met with a friend. We found another drug dealer, and within a few hours of having the ATF hold a gun in my face, I put more meth up my nose to fuel myself for another night of stealing and robbing. That night, we scouted near the hotel room since I now had no car. We walked a few miles away, and I climbed on top of the roof looking for scrap metal and wires and things to rip apart. Things slowed down, and I focused as I walked on the edge of this building two stories up. I heard a little movement in a vent I was prospecting for scrap metal to steal.

SWISH!!!! About a dozen birds jumped out of the fan and swarmed all around me and then flew up and away, almost knocking me off of the edge of the building. I became furious. I had had enough that night.

I went back and slept for about 4 hours, then woke up and started again. And that was it, what life consisted of. It was like the movie *Groundhog Day*, where Bill Murray wakes up every day to the same day and same routine. Drugs, stealing, getting caught, more traumatizing events every day and somehow figuring out a way to justify doing it all over again.

After the night of the ATF raid and my car getting impounded, I had been on a binge that kept me awake for about 2 weeks, with the exception of three or four nights where I slept for maybe 4 hours. We were out and about scouting for things to steal and pulled into Memorial Park at about mid-morning. My buddy, nicknamed "Superman," grabbed his knife and stepped out of the vehicle toward a red convertible. He raised the Buck knife and jabbed it into the top of an old lady's convertible.

For some reason, this scene was horrific to me. My conscience was breaking me down. I was feeling remorse for the first time in months. The old lady who owned the convertible, overweight and barely able to walk, did her best to run toward the car and yelled "Stop! Please stop!" as my friend snatched her purse from the front seat. Ducks was driving and laughing hysterically. Superman hopped into the car and we squealed away as quickly as possible.

My conscience was catching up with me; I couldn't help but picture that little old lady running toward her car and begging for him to stop. I caught a break in between my thoughts and heard Ducks and Superman in the front seat.

"We're going to Denver. Fuck this small-time shit!"

Ducks pushed the pedal to the floor and, like that, we were headed for the capital of Colorado. As we drove, each thought is filled with guilt and anguish. The voices in my head pierced my ears with each passing thought. My thoughts flooded my body, and I could feel the stress make every one of my muscles tense. My paranoia ran deep in my psyche—and there was no talking myself out of my psychosis at this point.

We stopped at a rest stop in Castle Rock and I picked up a flyer with a little cartoon in it, and I read it. It had a picture of God showing a man a glimpse of what his life could be through Him, and what it *actually* was.

His life without God was hellacious and full of stress and heartbreak. His life with Him, depicted in a photo of the man having a meal with his family, was him living to his potential.

The Bottom

The flyer reminded me of my childhood. What a peaceful life I could have had. It spoke to me in between my psychotic episodes. It made me feel something. Remorse. Something deep again, something I had forgotten.

I came back to the car and told them both we had to go back to Colorado Springs. Convincing two drug addicts to stray off of their path to get more drugs, and to take me to get help was nearly impossible, but I eventually talked them into taking me back to Colorado Springs. On the way back, I remember hearing the Fort Minor song "Where'd you go?". I had them drop me off in a random parking lot on Academy Blvd. at 11 o'clock in the morning, after I had called my mother to come pick me up. I gave my last $30 to another addict they had picked up along the way, and that was the end of this binge.

I was drinking a beer, not sure what time it was, as I waited for my mom. Summer was nearly over, and I had spent all of it drugging and robbing and driving myself into insanity and psychosis. This was the first time in my addiction that I had reached out and surrendered myself for help. I had cried only once after Xaq's funeral, but I felt like I could have cried for days. I held inside of me a heart full of pain from addiction and losing two of my best friends.

Where was I going? Who was I? I had to stop and figure things out. Only a few brief moments in my active addiction had I ever felt this clarity, moments when I knew I needed to ask for help or get clean, and I had never taken advantage of that vulnerability or weakness before. Now was the time. I was 18 and didn't know what way was down or up. For me, everywhere I went there was an elephant of pain in the room, and the elephant got bigger each time I chose not to cry or not to open up to someone. After a few months of that, my emotions imploded and started to turn into schizophrenia and psychosis. Hiding something so deep and big inside your mind will eventually fester and turn into an infection.

I saw my mother coming to my rescue. I set my beer on the curb and walked toward her car. I could feel my emotions building up and surfacing. She pulled up next to me, and I reached for the door. The schizophrenia dissipated, and my pain surfaced and shocked me back to reality. My whole world crumbled that day. Everything I had learned on the streets or before it all—as a kid or in the church or from school. Every belief structure I had. Every negative and every positive thought crumbled the second I closed the door to my mom's car and started bawling.

I had never cried like this in my life. Every thought about God, the devil, every single fiber of my being was shaken. This day will have forever changed me until the day I die. The intensity of this pain was unworldly. This was true rock bottom. This was Divine Intervention. This was my chaos and karma, but also my gift. My blessing and my curse all at the same time.

I confronted my evil that day. The details are blurry, but I remember the pain. They say emotional pain strikes the same part in your brain as physical pain, and this day was proof of that. I couldn't stop crying, and I couldn't stop it from becoming more intense every minute—18 years old and bawling like a baby in the front seat of my mother's car. Something finally blew up inside of me that had been festering for weeks. Something clicked inside of me that day and it still hasn't gone back to normal. This is what trauma feels like. A lot of bad things that happened in my life I have been able to forget and move past, but not this. I will remember this day and its pain for the rest of my life, like a curse. It's God's reminder of what taking your life for granted feels like. It's God's reminder of what you do when you choose to ignore all those missed opportunities, all those times you didn't choose help. All that free advice my mentors and loved ones gave me. I now pay for that advice with my pain.

According to my mother, I kept saying "Something is wrong, something is wrong!" I felt a pain in my chest that I can't describe. I might have had trouble breathing from all the crying and my chest contracting uncontrollably. My mom decided to take me to the hospital in case of an overdose. I continued crying in the E.R. until they got me a room. They put an IV in me to hydrate me, and after about 30 minutes I calmed down and started to become more conscious. Still in a deep fog, though, the first thing that came to mind was to get more drugs. After all that pain and all that trouble, and all the courage it took to ask for help, and now my solution was more drugs. My mother was in disbelief.

I look back and realize that this was not a physical overdose, but rather a mental overdose. And it left a scar on my brain that would last my lifetime. Every time I got high from that day forward would be different.

Every time I told a lie or did something I wasn't supposed to be doing, it would give me a deeper feeling of guilt and mental anguish. My paranoia was amplified, and it was now not the substance causing my insanity but the paranoia that had settled in my core belief structure. No, this was beyond a belief! This was a conviction. I was given the gift and curse of substance-induced psychosis. I was going to live years and years as a schizophrenic and I had no idea about how bad it would be for me. Three years of meth use and a lifetime of recovery from not only the addiction, but now mental illness.

The good news was I finally had a desire to stop doing drugs. A part of me was now going to start battling addiction. I would like to say that I won every battle from here out, but I didn't. I still had years of using and more bottoms to hit, even though I despised drugs and the chaos they brought. But I changed that day . . . I broke.

Recovery . . . In Pieces

I came to consciousness the more I was hydrated, and out of habit and lack of ability to reason I wanted more drugs. My parents left me in disgust. I walked about a block away from the hospital to a hiking trail. I stopped and looked down at my arm. I had track marks and bruises from shooting up, and now a huge bandage from the IV drip of sodium chloride.

I looked back at the hospital and thought about how bad what I went through was. I saw a few homeless people pass by and enjoyed the silence and the trees. It was a beautiful summer day. I hadn't noticed a good day in months. Two choices: back to insanity or try to recover.

I have to give sobriety a shot.

So, I did. This was the day I started my recovery. However, this was not the last day I used drugs.

My brain was being run by fear. I had felt the effects of brain damage and lack of brain chemicals from meth as well. I had no sense of empathy for other human beings, because of how much I had isolated myself. I felt I had no way to communicate with another human being. It started with feeling like no one had gone through things that were as bad as what I had been through. Maybe sometimes that was true, but I didn't give anyone a chance, because I wasn't giving myself a chance to live. I felt nothing but pain every day. Ironic that as much as I wanted to avoid it, it was all I could feel. No happiness or excitement even for potentially life-changing opportunities. Just apathy and self-hate.

I didn't want to use drugs. I was now aware that the side effects I was warned about for years were not a myth. But I had no other way to deal with my life. I couldn't handle any of my impulses or cravings. My emotions ran rampant and were unpredictable, even for me. And now I had mental illness; substance-induced psychosis was the sum of all my fears. It fed on my insecurities and fears. It lived inside of me. It was me, but it was someone else. I was not in control of my thoughts anymore. I had two different people inside of me. One was the Nate people knew. People loved this Nate. He was a good guy, easy to get along with, and a deep thinker. And the other was a demon. Narcissistic, self-loathing, and hidden in the dark. He was also a deep thinker and just as intelligent, only driven by fear and craving chaos.

My mind had almost come up with a dual personality in my head so that I could start having a conscience again and be able to see right from wrong. I do believe my brain developed this psychosis to put fear back into me and to respect reality's consequences more. I had lived so long with apathy and reckless decisions, tempting death and God to take me out of this world. Now I would be put in check.

Living in psychosis is both traumatic and petrifying. The strength of the drugs mixed with a single fearful thought would stop me in my tracks. I would be frozen in time when some of these disturbing thoughts would cross my mind. The whole world was moving around me at what felt like 100 miles per hour, while I was left stagnant and paralyzed, stuck in a ceaseless thought process that drove me insane.

I went back to the hospital and checked myself in with the nurse again. She was snide and rude with her comments. Her opinion on addiction and addicts was very transparent through her interaction with me. Since I had caused problems for them before, I could no longer get straight into detox and they made me wait. I waited and waited. I told them I needed sleep as I started to crash over and over.

I had no patience and was only familiar with impulse and fulfilling my primitive needs. After about three hours, they finally gave me a room to lie down in. It took me a while to get to sleep, but once I did I was out cold. A few hours later an ambulance arrived to drive me to detox. It was dark out now. They loaded me up, and I had a blanket around me. I looked out the window and noticed the pavement, turned yellow from the street lights. The only emotion I can remember feeling is exhaustion and emptiness, and some strange sort of relief. I felt a distant sense of peace in knowing I had finally made a rational choice. I made it to detox and was shown to my room.

As the door shut behind me, I could smell myself and I felt bad for my roommate. I had spent weeks sweating out meth, sweating from running, sweating from stress and paranoia. All of those long sunny days and long rainy nights soaked into the same pants and same shirt. These clothes have seen more in two weeks than most people do in a lifetime.

I laid down and fell into a deep sleep. I slept for about two days. I woke up once or twice and remember eating a banana and smoking a cigarette. When I smoked a cigarette, I remember hearing a man talk about his alcoholism and how it was destroying his life. I was interested and tried harder to listen. He started talking about his wife and their problems. My paranoia started to kick in. My psychosis would take his words and rearrange them in a different order. I heard what he was saying, but I started to believe it was directed at me. The nagging in the back of my head would distract from paying full attention to what he was saying, and every fifth word or so I would snap back from reality and think he was somehow talking about me. It's like I was falling in and out of reality and psychosis. This hurt me mentally. I finished my cigarette and went back to bed.

A day or two later, I called a friend to come pick me up out of detox. I called her because I had intentions of using, but when I landed myself in a tweaker pad, freshly out of detox, I found myself scared to use. This was a first.

The psychosis I knew I would fall into was intimidating, and I kind of liked the feeling of thinking straight and not living in fear. I spent a few minutes watching everyone else get high before she took me to Tim's house, the same Tim I used meth with the first time. They were strung out there too. Tim's mother stopped by and somehow a fight had ensued, and Tim had kicked the sliding glass door off the tracks and made a mess everywhere. I don't remember how, but I made my way home. I talked to my parents briefly before I made my way to my old bedroom and fell asleep again for a long period.

I woke up sometime the next day, and my parents and I talked about getting into treatment. I was open to it this time and wanted help. My psychosis was nearly gone now. One of the perks of being young is quick recovery. We picked out a program called Teen Challenge. But after a few days at my parents' house, the memory of how painful my last binge was started to dissolve in my mind and my cravings came back, and I found myself back at the dealer's house.

I don't remember what set me off to go to the dealer's house. It could have been something very small and simple. It could have been an argument or something else that was stressful. Or it could have been the opposite—too much boredom and downtime. It could have been sitting in sadness for more than an hour. It was so easy, way too easy, to get meth again. After the most traumatic events in my life, I still chose to use.

The story was the same. I got high, and it felt great for a few minutes. Then the psychosis ensued. I made it a few days and barely survived this time. On the last day of this binge, I took a shot of cocaine that almost landed me in the E.R. This was the last shot in the bag. My buddy asked me to share it, but I told him no. My selfishness would render a grave consequence: I remember seeing everything go black and my heart started slowing down.

Keep your heart beating, Nate. Ride this out. Breath by breath, just don't stop. Wait for the darkness to go away.

Repeat these words. And then you wait... Hopefully your body processes the drug before your heart stops and your soul lets go. I eventually came back to a twisted reality.

This incident reminded me of a passage in *Trainspotting*, where the character battles an overdose. Everything fades except for your soul and the primitive part of your brain. You talk to the primitive part and remind it that it needs to keep your heart beating. Reality is within eyesight, but you don't have the strength to hold on to it.

I hitched a ride and made it back to my hometown, and almost home. Despite almost overdosing, a few hours later I used meth a few more times. It was just too easy, and I didn't know how to say no. Every room in the house had people using meth in it. People were shooting meth in one room and smoking meth in another. People were tweaking out and smoking cigarettes and having some bullshit conversation downstairs. I needed someone to talk to, but everyone was too high. I was too high.

I fought my psychosis until it drove the fear deep into me and it couldn't be handled anymore. I left without saying goodbye and walked about 4 miles to get home and escape. The voices whispered in my ears and chased me home to whole way. My mind made up paranoid theories to keep it occupied. At this point in psychosis, even though I was paranoid, my thoughts were still somewhat smooth. Not rational, but my mind flowed. I didn't block things out. My emotions were painful, and my mind was at times, but the psychosis was just there. It was still kind of tucked away in my mind.

Each car that passes is messing with you. They are looking at you. They are talking about you. They are all after you

This time, the detox wasn't as easy. Most come-downs off of meth are nothing but sleep and eating. This time, I had given myself insomnia. The drug was out of my system, but I couldn't rest. My psychosis had become so strong that it wouldn't let me sleep now. I sat in my head, going insane, and moaning in agonizing mental pain. At one point, I sat up and was mustering the energy to slam my head on the corner of my bed so I could go unconscious.

Go hard, Nate. Do what you have to do. Kill the pain!!!

My father woke up around 4 a.m. for work and heard me crying and moaning, making whatever other insufferable noises he could hear. He came to my room and very simply and calmly told me to go to work with him, and he promised it would help. Ninety-nine percent of me did not want to go, but that 1% was lonely, hurt, and scared enough to go—the small part of the old Nate that was left. He let me smoke cigarettes and listen to music in his van, even though he didn't smoke.

I opened up to my dad about some things and eventually started feeling better. The psychosis would go away whenever I would talk to others. It would take about 5 minutes of my talking, and hearing what I was saying, before I reached a reasonable place of consciousness and before my words would make sense. Sometimes I wouldn't talk for days while I was on meth, and I would travel deep into the chasms of my mind and find a psychosis that would give me permission to remain silent and isolate from the world and reality. When the insanity finally got the better of me, I would talk just because I felt uncomfortable, and most of the time my words wouldn't make sense.

I started going with my father to work regularly, and there were other times when I can remember being in my dad's work van and wading through memories and thoughts in my head. They moved so slowly and wouldn't process because they were traumatic. I knew that, because I was an addict, I was going to react to things based on emotions instead of rational thought. So I would sit and try to work these things out in my mind. It took forever because I thought I was "thought broadcasting" and had to be careful about what I said with the voice in my head. I believed I had to paint a certain picture for others around me. When I thought I had figured something out or felt I had processed something, I would picture it blow up like a firework in my head. I was literally insane.

After that first day with my father, I decided to get into treatment ASAP. I spent about a week with my parents before going in. I got back into writing poems and short stories and saw some sober friends who stopped by to show support. I saw my old friend Jacob, who I used to play baseball and football with. It meant the world to me. After a few days, the psychosis wore off again. Ryan came over, and we had a deep talk, as we usually did. The subject came up of suicide and of how hard our lives had been that summer. We joked about holding a metal pole in the middle of a field and being struck by lightning, and how original a suicide idea that would be. The casualness of our conversation is disturbing in retrospect, but that was all we knew at the time. Just then, we saw a lightning bolt strike, down the mountain a little way, and make a loud crack that was stunning. "That one hit the ground!" Ryan said. A day later, we found out that another Woodland Park kid had died from being struck on a soccer field by the lightning bolt we saw hit the ground.

Rehab #2

Even though I had spent the week at my parents' house clean, I was still deep in the chaos of my mind and addiction. I was not even close to being a rational or reasonable human being. My bipolar up-and-down, cold-and-hot mood swings dominated my decisions. My parents drove me out to Kansas to complete a treatment program in hopes of turning things around. It was on a farm in a rural community. When I showed up, they made me throw my cigarettes away, which I wasn't happy about. I had been off meth for only about a week and a half and now they wanted me to quit smoking cigarettes? Strike one.

When I began my check-in, I heard the staff members refer to themselves as sisters and brothers, and it quickly became apparent that this was a religious-based program. I had spent my whole life in a Christian home and I now resented organized religion. Strike two.

I ate dinner and rested before the next day. I never could get enough sleep. I could sleep probably 15 hours in a day before I even thought about being productive. They woke me up early and had everyone start school around 8 a.m. I was irritated the first day and tried to take naps during class and was constantly bothered to stay awake and study the Bible. School consisted of studying the Bible and learning verses. I had no desire to do any of these things and just wanted to sleep. A lot of the kids there hadn't done a lot of drugs and just had what I considered to be mild attitude problems. Most of them were younger and were not mentally tainted as I was. *This program wasn't ready for an IV meth user in this amount of pain.*

We spent the rest of the day farming in the heat, and in the evening attended a church service. I don't remember much about these times. My brain was still foggy. I remember hating the program. I remember seeing a pretty girl in church. She wasn't a part of the program; she was just a member of the community. I saw no pain in her. I saw her smiling and having fun. I saw her laughing and interacting with another boy in church. I became envious and spiteful. *I have to sit here, in this substandard program, and farm like a slave all day and go to Bible school and be told there is a God who loves me?*

After all the bullshit I've seen, they want me to study the Bible? Whoa, whoa!!! I don't even believe in God anymore. When I do, I hate him. Middle finger to the sky! Have these sheltered, pathetic fools seen what I've seen? Have you seen evil before? I have!

One night, when I'd been strung out for days, after my first ATF raid, I closed my eyes and saw a demon. He was dark and blurry. He entered my mind that night, and he hasn't left since. He sits there in the back of my head and scratches on the walls of my brain until it bleeds. He laughs at my pain and tells me what to think. He gets more powerful each time I get high. *Where is God now? Was He there to rescue me when I was being violated by my babysitter or when she was violated by whoever hurt her? Was he there when my best friend hung by a rope around his neck, squirming and gasping for air?*

I couldn't relate to any of the kids or staff there, and the religious structure was more than I could accept. I had one good conversation with another admitted client there after the day was done, but not much more than that.

The next morning, the staff tried to wake me up. I ignored them and milked another 10 minutes of sleep. They tried again, and my rage erupted. I awoke from bed and the demon accompanied me. I cursed at every staff member to cross my path. I folded my sheet in anger and never stopped my tongue from lashing out. I struck deep and used the lowest insults I could. I yelled about how I didn't care about their religious bullshit and how they wouldn't let me sleep and come down properly. I tried my best to make them hurt like I hurt. I spewed venom from my insides. I was toxic. I was full of hate and rage. This was who I had become. This is what my pain had come to. *I'm not the kid who went to church every Sunday. I'm not the kid who went to New York to play baseball. Whoever that child was is bruised, broken, and left behind. I am only concerned about what I want.* This is who I had become.

The drugs were gone, but my addiction was still present. The evil and pain in me still lingered. After problems became too much for my mind, it would erupt. Even though I wanted help *one* day, my mentality could flip 180 degrees the next day. I had discovered I was two different people. Two different sets of opinions, two different consciousnesses.

Back on the Streets

After cussing out the staff, I demanded my stuff back and told them I was leaving. I left in a storm and set out for the streets. I had taught myself how to survive without money or a home and knew I would have to steal to support myself. I walked for a few miles and ended up downtown on a Thursday. It was surprisingly busy. I went up to the first people I saw smoking and asked for a cigarette. On the way, I heard them talking about crystal meth. My psychosis told me they were talking about me.

They know I'm the crazy kid from Woodland Park, Colorado.

They ended up giving me half a pack of smokes. I was set for a while. I smoked and roamed downtown. The night fell and I knew I needed a place to sleep, so I found a school bus station. I pried the door open on a bus in the far back corner of the lot and slept in the back of the bus. I knew they wouldn't use this bus for anything or I would wake up if they intended to use it. The bus's floor was rough and unforgiving—an immediate consequence of my choice to leave the treatment facility. I remember looking at the stars in a strange state of peace, no longer emotionally distraught by conflict.

Dysfunction was normal in my life now. I missed Xaq. I missed Morgan. I'm still not over Sarah Jane. Just hearing about the kid being struck by lightning on the soccer field reminded me even more of tragedy. The pain is always in my mind. I think about them constantly, and I feel sorry for myself. I miss them. I miss all those I've lost. But of all of the people I've lost in my life, the one I miss most is me.

I woke up the next morning, lit up a smoke, and started my trek to Walmart. It was farther than expected. It ended being a 4- or 5-mile walk. I made it by noon. I walked in and grabbed a cart. I grabbed some plastic bags from an empty checkout counter. I went through the aisles and grabbed some soups and Gatorade and put them into the plastic bags. I roamed around and made my way to the front, and with the food already loaded into the bags, it looked like I had paid for them. I made my way back to the bus station.

On the long walk to the bus station, I passed a dirty street and saw syringe lying on the ground. I wanted to pick it up and check the cap for dope, but decided not to. Once I finally made it back to the bus station, I used a rock to bash open the top of a can, so I could eat cold soup. I drank Gatorade and water and walked around town. I made my way to a pay phone and called my parents to let them know I was alive. They agreed to buy me a bus ticket and they talked to the staff at the facility and convinced them to give me a ride to the bus station in two days.

I spent the next few days walking around, indulging in my insane thoughts with no intervention and no interference. We've all seen those lonely homeless people walking around the downtown area of any big city, talking to themselves, dirty, lost. In a brief moment, you wonder what their story is. Maybe you judge them, maybe you don't. Maybe you engage them in conversation or maybe you keep as far away as possible. They talk to themselves, and you can see them doing it from a block away. Once you get closer you hear what they're talking about; sometimes it's unintelligible and sometimes it's a very true statement or philosophy. Most of the time, their conversation is too deep to dive into. Sometimes their babbling is something you could relate to if you had time to ask about their thought process. But it probably just sounds like rambling nonsense. One thing is for sure, you know they have a long, unique, and peculiar story about how they got there. I was that crazy person you see roaming around aimlessly—just roaming around in my own little broken world.

Home Again

I had made it home. Again. Somehow not dead, again. I still had a desire to stay clean. But still felt a festering pain inside. My sobriety failed once again. I can't remember how long it took. I didn't keep track or get shocked when I relapsed anymore. Maybe a week. Maybe I injected, maybe not. Maybe I snorted it and I felt like I did okay because I didn't inject. I stayed up, beat off, wrote nonsense in my notebooks, and reached out for help to friends who were just as broken as I was. I lived this way. I was conditioned. The psychosis came back every time and beat my ass. Each binge would be worse than the last. I thought I had made progress because I was an on-and-off addict instead of an everyday user now.

Shannah had moved back from Texas, and I was still using with her father. I was different from when we first met, and even more distant. I felt like a freak and like everyone could see through me and see what I was thinking. She loved me, but she knew I was broken, so we couldn't have a relationship. We talked about it one day, though. She explained her feelings, and I told her I felt like she was mine. Our conversation was cut short when several of her friends came over. I left the room for a few minutes and when I came back one of the guys had his arm around her. I sat down and stared at the two of them for about 30 minutes. They passed the weed bowls around and mingled and laughed and socialized, as I sat there in anger.

I barked at both of them in my head, thinking they could hear me. The louder I yelled and cursed, the more fun they had and the more they laughed together. I just knew they could hear what I was thinking, and I knew they were mocking me.

I'm such a low piece of shit. I don't deserve to be recognized.

Eventually, they left and passed me over. Shannah walked by me with no words.

My drug dealer had been robbing cars the night before and found an I.D. I could use to buy alcohol. Amazingly, the picture looked exactly like me. Strung out from the night before and hurt, I knew this was the perfect chance to break it in. I went to the liquor store and bought my first 22-ounce beer at age 18. I went back to Shannah's house, and somehow her younger brother had gotten a hold of some meth. We smoked it and listened to the song "Running" from Tupac."

My mood was now balanced from the alcohol and meth. I was high from the meth, but my nerves were perfectly leveled. I wasn't happy though. God knows I didn't deserve that. I was just content with my depression.

My mother picked me up, and I had made it home to come down. As soon as I got home, my parents left to go to dinner with some friends. There I sat in the house, all alone, processing my hurt from the day: Shannah leaving me for someone else. My meth addiction. My weakness and failure in sobriety. Binge after binge kicking my ass all over town. I was ready to give up. Time to throw in the towel. How much am I supposed to handle?

I went downstairs and grabbed my father's .357 Magnum from the walk-in closet. Beautiful gun. I loaded it up with one bullet and cocked it. Tears welled up in my eyes, and I sobbed. I prayed. I cried out for help, but no one came. No one called me on my phone. Ironic, since I thought there were cameras all over my house with people watching me. Reluctantly, I stuck the gun in my mouth.

I don't want this. I can't stop though. It's just time. It just makes sense now.

I understand why people kill themselves. It's not crazy. It's sad, but it's not that crazy.

Minutes go by. My finger is not on the trigger. I'm arguing with myself over it. I lower the gun. Then I put it in my mouth again. This time more firmly, aggressively. But nope. Still can't do it.

Eventually I gave up and unloaded the gun and put it back. Now I'm just angry. Living against my will: what kind of bullshit is this? I went to bed angry that night and loaded with fear of having to wake up the next day. At least the meth would wear off by then.

I woke up the next morning feeling a lot better. Still tired and grumpy, but not suicidal. I didn't think much about it. My psychosis didn't allow for much reflection or rational thought about the past. I was too busy now running from my own thoughts and overanalyzing other things. My mind was busy from the second I woke up. I had about 30 seconds to a minute in the morning before the voices in my head woke up with me.

That minute is nice. I forget who I am and what I've been through. I am naturally myself. Never for long though.

I spent that day eating and taking a nap, trying to come down off a small meth bender. Before too long, I need to use. Anything: weed, alcohol, cocaine, mushrooms. I called up a friend, Chester, to see if I can hitch a ride to Colorado Springs to go smoke pot with another friend, John. Chester picked me up around 4 o'clock. We set off to take a trip to Colorado Springs. From the second I get into the car, people are talking. I don't pay attention to what they are saying, because I think they are messing with my mind.

We got about 5 miles into the drive when I heard them say "Travis killed himself last night."

Wait! Did I hear right?

"Travis who? Travis Strausser?" Yep, that's right.

The kid I'd known since kindergarten. Played sports with him my whole life. We used to antagonize each other and get into fights about three or four times a school year, and then be best friends the next day after a fist fight. I smoked pot my very first time with this young man. We used to skateboard together. He killed himself. He's dead now. I hadn't seen him in about a year, since I started to get heavy into meth.

"How did he do it?" I asked.

"Shot himself last night, Nate," Chester replied.

I said nothing. I just sat there. I'm supposed to believe that we both had guns in our mouths the exact same night? Possibly even the exact same moments?

Bullshit. Everyone is watching the cameras in my house and saw what I did, so they are mind-fucking me to keep me from doing it again. They know what I did last night. They're mind-fucking me. Just like they did when that kid supposedly got struck by lightning.

Not a minute after I was talking about killing myself in a field with a metal pole getting struck by lightning, a young kid dies from a lightning bolt.

Yeah, okay. They're mind-fucking me and it's not right. It's evil. They mess with me to try to change me. Or. . . am I just in psychosis and my life really is this crazy?

I got to the Springs, and Shannah and Ray were there at my friend's house. They must have heard about me losing another friend and didn't want me to go on another suicide mission, like I did with Xaq's passing. We got stoned, and I felt a little better for the moment. My voices slowed down, and I almost felt like I had control. Shannah took me outside to talk. She didn't apologize, and she tried to talk about Travis. I just remember thinking I wanted to slap her in the face.

She's lucky her dad is as tough as he is, and I'm as passive as I am.

I made it through that night at my friend's house. I had $60 saved up from coming back from Kansas. My parents had sent me too much money for the bus ticket, and I saved the rest for myself. I knew exactly where this money was going this morning. I had new pain to cover. More loss I didn't want to deal with. More death. More rationale for psychosis. What a perfect day to inject meth.

I made my way to my dealer's house. He was staying with someone named Maggie. She was disabled and overweight. A single mom and a meth addict. I tried to come over when her daughter was at school or asleep, but it didn't always work out that way. We had no business being in this home. This day, her daughter was at school. The drugs were already there and I didn't have to wait. I had clean syringes, and I had no one bothering me. I did my first shot.

This is good dope.

It rushed to my head with heat, the only thing I've known to relieve my tension. I had a casual conversation with my dealer and his girl. I contemplated a second shot. I know what happens on my second shots; the insanity becomes uncontrollable. It's always there, but I told myself I could manage on the first shot. I didn't want to shoot up again, but I didn't know how not to.

The conversation was starting to bore me, and I couldn't think of anything else to do. I don't want to go have fun while I'm high. I don't want to draw or write like every other tweaker. I want to shoot up. So I loaded the second shot. Even bigger than the first. It didn't even get me high, no more feel-good chemicals to release. Instead, I went insane, like I knew I would.

It started with me choosing to be silent, lazy, with my mind losing interest in reality. I was scared of people, so I didn't want to talk because I was depressed and not high enough. I felt dirty; my mind felt dirty. So many days of this. So many days of toxicity through meth and unhealthy thoughts. I sunk back into the wall and felt chaos ensue, going out of control again.

I'm not me. Nate no longer is available. You can talk to meth and psychosis now.

The voices did my talking for me, and I convinced myself that the voices in my head somehow talk aloud when I'm not talking, which meant people could hear what I was thinking. No, not just a small funny little trip on a meth bender; this had become a strong belief and I couldn't be convinced otherwise. It was as if I were watching from the sidelines, out of body.

I sunk back into the wall. The chaos was all around, not only inside my mind but also with the ones I was hanging out with. I saw them arguing, and I thought it was because of me. Maybe it was. My silence always seemed to create tension.

Their arguing got louder and one of them broke a plate on the counter. More yelling. I heard about every third word in their argument and somehow thought their anger was projected at me, like they were doing this to mentally torment me. They were angry with me, but took it out on each other to get at me and raise my anxiety. They were good at it too! They hate me, and they were filled with rage, but they wouldn't even look at me.

The drug dealer smacked his girlfriend. I stayed dormant for a second, in shock, then said, "Chill the fuck out, Rick!" I thought I said this loudly, but I was far back into a hole, and there was no confidence behind my words. No one takes me seriously. The fighting continued and I finally stepped in between them and separated them. Trying to battle them and the voices in my head was a challenge and made me more timid. He went into the living room and she stayed in the kitchen. She wanted to cry. I still somehow thought they were mad at me.

I called a friend to pick me up. I'd been there too long and I was too high. The high was wearing off, too, which meant the psychosis and voices were going to come on stronger. I left the house and walked down the street in the direction my friend would be coming to pick me up. It was sunny, but cold outside at midday, and a lot of cars and activity were around the neighborhood, which is a recipe for disaster in the mind of a schizophrenic. I tried to evaluate what I looked like. My face would move around uncontrollably since I thought my mouth was speaking my thoughts aloud.

Do I look suspicious? I don't think I do. I look too normal. These people have no idea what it's like inside my head.

"Why are you so quiet, Nate?" I was asked all the time, which would piss me off. If only they knew how loud it was inside my head. Here I was looking the most normal, yet I was the most insane.

Here comes my friend. He sees me. He sees me walking around in my broken little world.

Chapter 4

Psychosis and Going over the Edge

"The Edge . . .There is no honest way to explain it because the only people who really know where it is are the ones who have gone over."

— **<u>Hunter S. Thompson</u>, *<u>Hell's Angels: A Strange and Terrible Saga</u>***

A few months went by of my on-and-off drug use. When I returned from Kansas, I had some hope of staying clean. That didn't last long.

I wouldn't use drugs *every* day, because I recognized the deterioration to my mental health that daily use brought. So, I created a routine—a repeating cycle—to keep the drug use under control.

Step 1: After about 3 to 7 days, I would start to feel better from my last binge and begin to think more clearly.

Step 2: With my clearer thinking, feelings would come back, underlying issues that I couldn't identify at the surface. I developed a poor attitude and justifications for why I didn't have to act like a normal, functional human being. I developed a chip on my shoulder for all the pain I've endured.

Step 3: Small problems would arise, or I was unable to cope with feelings.

Step 4: I would then leave my parents' home, a drug-free, healthy environment, and acquire money by any means possible, whether it be lying to parents/friends, or selling drugs, or stealing

Step 5: I would get high, feel good for 15 minutes, indulge in insanity, and deny how bad my psychosis was for about 4 hours. Then I would spend the rest of the binge too petrified to do anything about it, for fear of what the actual solution might be.

Step 6: A few days would fly by quicker than I could keep track and I'd realize my psychosis was unmanageable, and that I am broken. Sleep deprivation, feelings of guilt, anger, malnourishment, and sadness overwhelmed me. I contemplated getting a psychiatrist or going into treatment. Sometimes, I would open up to my parents or friends and be vulnerable, but I was still under the influence.

Step 7: I would call friends or family and find my way home, riding out the psychosis until I could sleep. Hopefully, I would fall asleep before I contemplated or attempted suicide.

Step 8: Repeat the above, only do it better next time . . .

I learned later that there are clinical terms for the insanity I indulged in—terms like "thought broadcasting." This is the delusion that your thoughts are being broadcast and others can hear them. This belief put me in constant fight-or-flight mode, like I had to try to control what my deepest emotions or thoughts were. Can you imagine what it would be like to hear every single thought you have come out loud? I felt naked and vulnerable 24/7. It caused me a lot of pain and mental anguish. What I did with those thoughts was the only thing I *could* control. How I felt was impulsive and unavoidable. Can you imagine having to watch what you think at every moment, every time someone says something, for fear that people can read your mind? It's a ridiculous concept, but to a meth addict it is very real and sickening.

"Gang stalking," the belief that you are being harassed or persecuted by a mob or community of people, also played a role in my delusional mind. Many tweakers believe they are constantly being stalked, and I thought I was too. I thought that everyone was literally out to get me. It is a real thing for some people, but in the case of most meth addicts, it's a hallucination and/or delusion. In my case, I thought others would harass me with their words in reaction to hearing my thoughts being broadcast out loud. This was constant chaos, and my brain was constantly driven by fear.

This is what it's like to be schizophrenic. A brain with meth-associated psychosis shows the same type of activity as that of a schizophrenic. Meth-induced psychosis is particularly unique in the length of time the psychosis will last, despite discontinued meth use. It feels as though you will never get better. Some call it "the fog." It may last for months or years, and even after that it sometimes comes back.

Before I hit rock bottom in my mother's car that day, my psychosis wasn't as bad as it had become now. Even though I was paranoid before, I didn't feel like I had to fight with myself. Now, since I believed I had a split personality that spoke aloud I spent all of my time fighting myself. If I would have quit drugs, I might have recovered better, but I didn't. The voices in my head would say nastier things or they might even scream. It made me flinch sometimes it was so disturbing. It was like little pin pricks inside my brain. Sometimes I would get too high and I would insult people in my brain and say the worst possible things imaginable, as though I had no control. Even people I loved or felt connected to would be a target, like some alter ego had hijacked my brain.

The voices rarely stopped while I was awake, unless I did just the right amount of meth to feel comfortable with myself for a short time, or I got drunk enough to numb out the pain of the inner voices and screams. What it really boiled down to was lack of confidence and the incineration of my ego. It was as though the good part of me had died and what was coming through was a conflicting split personality. I didn't have the courage to stand up to the bad part of myself, so it naturally took over because it was unopposed.

If I was fortunate enough to tame my psychosis, I would still have to deal with anhedonia, the state of feeling no pleasure in life. No joy. Everything is gray. Being a dimension away from reality in a dark state. I think part of the reason I came up with the psychosis was to make my life more interesting and less gray. You can see everyone around you smiling or having fun, and there you are in your own little world of nothingness. This is why some addicts choose to self-sabotage, because to feel pain is better than to feel nothing. This is why I cut myself. This is why I hurt myself. This is why I pitied myself. Being insane might have been better then feeling nothing.[9]

This was my life, and it went on like this seemingly forever. With the decline of my mental health, my judgement for dosing my drugs became careless as well. That and the fact that I couldn't stand living like this and would have rather died.

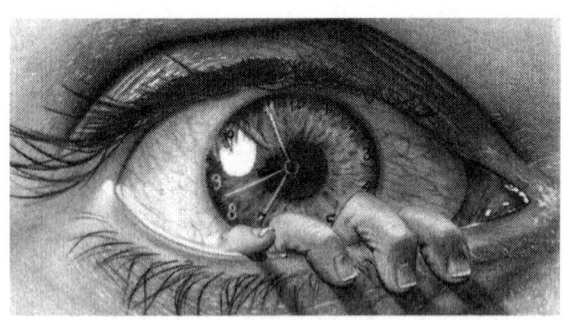

A day came when I almost overdosed on mixing morphine, meth, and alcohol. I was silent in the back of my dealer's car for hours and no one thought anything was wrong until I started vomiting uncontrollably. I couldn't talk, so they pulled over to a gas station and got me food. The food helped soak up the alcohol, but I still couldn't talk. They rushed me to my parents' house and helped me to the front door, and left me as quickly as possible, probably so they could avoid charges if I died. I crawled up the stairs and into my room. Despite my exhaustion, I couldn't sleep. I think that if the meth hadn't been in my system, my heart might have stopped that day after I passed out.

---

[9] https://throughtheeyesofi.com/cropped-cropped-imagesagaskboy-jpg/

Dark Ritual

Suicide was always on my mind—literally every day. I thought about it all the time. When the drugs and psychosis would win, I might make an attempt at it. Or at least a cry for help. A few weeks after my near overdose, I found myself alone in my room and strung out again. I had talked myself into a deep dark depression and then began to hack at my arm with an X-Acto knife to relieve the tension from this darkness.

This is what I deserve.

It started with just a few cuts. It was not enough, though. I craved something more extreme, so I cut harder.

I'm ready to die.

The cuts got deeper and harder.

Keep going and you'll feel light-headed. You need to hit an artery. Go deeper.

This now became hacking, not cutting. I raised my hand about a foot from my forearm and struck down with self-hatred.

Repeat. Repeat. Keep going until you get light-headed.

I did this for about 30 minutes—crying and hacking at my arm—until I figured out I wasn't going to die. During this disturbing period, my father came and knocked on the door.

"Nate? You okay, buddy?" he asked.

Lie. Lie Lie. "Yep, I'm good," I replied, holding back pain.

I had become so good at lying. I continued to dissect my arm. When I finished, it was bloody, and my whole forearm was missing layers of skin.

This will leave scars.

The thought of having these scars made me regretful. After all I have done and been through, I was bound to have regrets. I'm not a normal person who can say he lived his life with no regrets, but then I don't believe the people who say they have none. I regret not helping Xaq more. If I had helped Xaq out, he wouldn't have died. If Xaq hadn't died, Morgan wouldn't have died. I don't think she would have gotten as drunk that night and I don't think she would have decided to drive while intoxicated. Travis wouldn't have died either. Suicide and seeking death wouldn't have been as socially acceptable as it was for my friends, and it would have been harder for them to do. And I wouldn't have been as high, and I wouldn't have been sitting there hacking my arm and ripping my flesh with an X-Acto knife.

This reminded me of the time I carved "junkie" into my arm and Xaq saw it and tried to help me. I was so focused on myself and my addiction that I didn't realize he needed help. I was so self-centered, and I had no help to offer.

I regretted stealing almost every time after I did it. I regretted sticking a needle in my arm, and before that, I regretted ever smoking meth out of that bong.

How did I get this way? This all happened so fucking quickly. I'm only 18 years old.

I was playing baseball and football and part of a loving family, what seemed like just yesterday. I had supportive and healthy friends. How could I throw this away? I don't want to throw this away, but it's too late now. I'm in too deep and this is how the rest of life will go. I will live broken.

A few weeks went by, and the scars healed. I covered them with long sleeves until they healed. When I was alone, I would run my finger along the bumpy edge of the scabs. I didn't want to show anyone, because that would mean they would help me and give me empathy. No thanks. I don't deserve that. I got deeper into meth almost like I had been in the summer, which meant using everyday instead of going through small benders and recovering. Fall turned into winter and the months passed with no hope of change. No signs of God, or none that I could grasp. I needed something big to help me. I needed a miracle.

I still lived with my parents at this time, and I noticed my father's diabetic episodes getting worse. His blood sugar would fall dangerously low, and he wouldn't even be able to make it up the stairs to the kitchen to get food. He would fall often, and flail around on the floor and scream while trying to get up. I would be awakened by what sounded like an animal being hurt. The screams were loud and high-pitched and disturbing. They weren't my father. I would walk downstairs and see him flailing around and trying to get up. Sometimes he would fall over and crack his head on the edge of something. He didn't seem to feel it. My mother and I would try to talk to him, and he would look up with a blank stare on his face. Sometimes he would respond with nonsense or some smart-ass comment in his boggled frame of mind. It was sad. I would wake up, try to get him into his chair, get him some food or glucose tablets, spend 20 minutes forcing something into him to get his sugar up, and then go upstairs and cry as I went to sleep.

I ended up moving in with Ray, who had recently left his girlfriend for a different girl who was an addict too. I was feeling somewhat good and was gaining a small bit of control over my psychosis, or so I thought. I knew the amount of meth I would be up against while moving into a tweaker pad, so I did my best to act like a professional tweaker and not lose my mind. Ray had picked me up from a friend's house because he said that the house was a dump and was going to be trouble. It was raided a week later by a SWAT team.

Ray's house was much calmer and less chaotic. He and his new woman had jobs, and kids were there half the time, so we had to have some structure and respect. I wasn't injecting either, just smoking and snorting—a nice way to tell myself I was doing better than I actually was.

I somehow managed to smoke even more meth then I had in my entire life. It was always around. Ray made sure I would stay high. I had no money and nothing to offer, but he would feed me, gave me my own room, and supported my habit, asking nothing in return. I smoked all the weed I wanted and got drunk almost every day, too. When I got too tweaked, I would be sure to level out my high with alcohol. Alcohol was my savior some days. I would get lost in the psychosis and meth smoke, and alcohol would pull me out. I would get a false sense of confidence back and start talking and communicating. It got to the point that I needed to have alcohol, or I had no way to communicate. I wouldn't open up. I would sit there for days in silence getting high and not sleeping. Ray would buy liquor especially for me when he noticed me going silent.

Despite my problems, when the kids were present, I held my composure. I had to be strong. I would never want this life for any kid, and I didn't want them to ever see through me because that would crack the image of who they thought I was. I loved who the kids thought I was: A nice, mature young man. It reminded me of who I should have been. And deep down somewhere, I was that guy. I WAS who they thought I was. Meth was only the surface of who I was. All those terrible things I did or saw weren't the real me. I played video games with them and did my best to be cool around them. As much as they looked up to me, they still didn't deserve to be around this lifestyle. I felt vain because I wasn't clean. Everything seemed vain when I was high. I did things only to cover my own ass or to support my addiction.

The weeks went on. I did my best to progress. I even enrolled in community college and applied for a job at an Italian restaurant. Ray and his girlfriend would give me rides to school or to work.

I remember snorting a couple of huge lines in the bathroom at school before computer class. I knew one girl from high school, and she always tried to talk to me, but I had nothing to say.

My interest was still in English and writing, and my English class had all girls and me. I didn't talk to any of them; I didn't show any interest. I fantasized about one of them being able to get me to open me up, asking me about my problems and wanting to help me. In my mind, that was one of the only things that could fix me was love. I was right but gravely mistaken on where that love had to come from.

I quickly dismissed this inspirational fantasy. I wrote one or two papers in that class before dropping out. I think I even did okay on them. On one occasion, I showed up to class without my backpack. About half way to class I realized I had forgotten it and decided to show up on time, rather than being late and going back for my backpack. The teacher threw me out, since I didn't have anything to work with. I never went back.

Fiercer Demons

My psychosis was starting to come on strong again. This time, my mind knew all of tricks to deter it. I would play games with myself inside of my head to keep my insanity busy, but ironically that's the reason I was crazy. I was still in belief that others could hear my thoughts aloud too. This put me in constant mental panic. Constant. Never ceasing. Never easing. Never relaxing. Never dormant...panic. The monster was awake every second that I was, and it got worse with every bowl I would smoke and every line I would snort. It became harder and harder to talk.

Most of my memories from Ray's house are of sitting on the bed, smoking huge amounts of meth and never saying a word. Talking was painful to me. Any time I had to communicate I would have to psyche myself up for a minute before breaking my silence. I had to force words out, and I always thought I sounded petty. I hated the sound of my voice. I hated my helplessness.

You're stupid. You're dumb. You're legally insane. You'll have flashbacks for the rest of your life. Everyone is mind-fucking you. You have no peace.

I lost my job for obvious reasons. My mind would run rampant, and I couldn't focus while trying to work or function normally. I would stay locked in my inner prison and let the voices in my head run their chaos. There were multiple voices now; they would argue and they would speak for me. And since they did the talking there was no reason for me to. Here I was, completely broken and hurt, just needing to grab a hold of someone for help. I started to inject with Ray again. Eventually, I couldn't get drunk enough to talk with anybody. The meth was overpowering me.

Can't they hear me? No, they can't bring attention to my voices or it will encourage me to stay crazy. They hear me. They hear my thoughts. Why is this so funny to them? Is this a sick joke? Did you hear me just say I wanted to die? Why the fuck are they laughing? I have to talk. I don't want to talk. I am nothing. I need a cigarette. But this will cut the oxygen from my head, and I can't think straight.

Time to get high. Here comes the bowl. Ahhhh, yessss!. My medication. This will bring me out of the hole. I have to smoke enough to motivate me to talk and communicate, and work out my problems, and figure this out. I need the meth; it helps. Ah, here comes another hit. Here we go . . . I'm going to talk . . . Nope, I'll wait until the bowl is finished. Last hit; here we go . . . I'm still not high. I can't talk. Oh fuck, I'm falling. I'm in a hole. I'm too high.

"Can I have a cigarette?" I would ask. They would give. I would go silent again. Maybe I'd talk. Most of the time, it wouldn't make sense.

"Quit talking crazy, boy!" Ray would try to joke around with me and brighten my thoughts and mood. It never worked. I was unreachable.

Nate's not here anymore; you can speak with meth.

The liquor would come around, and I would drink until I passed out. If I was lucky, I'd open up a bit. Then I'd wake up, go downstairs, and start the psychosis ritual again—go downstairs and get smoked out with meth. I'd talk for a bit until I started getting high.

Use the meth. Use the meth to come out of the hole. A mental hole. I can't get out because I have to ask for help. I don't want to ask. I just want to be normal. The meth will help medicate me, because I have a strong chemical imbalance.

"Can I have a cigarette?" I ask. "Yeah, Nate, of course, have anything you want, boy." Ray always tried to make me feel welcome.

He's being sarcastic. He does mind. They hate me. I'm so broken. I'm so broken. I'm 25 percent retarded. I heard someone say it a while back. They said I'm brain-damaged 25 percent. I'm fucking stupid. Talk more, stupid. You're dumb. You can't hold a conversation. This proves you're brain damaged. You have holes in your brain and now you live in them. You have no expression. You never will. No brain chemistry to be normal. This will last the rest of your life. This is what you get for Xaq dying. This is what you get. God hates you. Everyone hates you.

After long periods of enduring mental warfare, I would go hide in my room and think cameras were watching me. Watching my insanity. Maybe even projecting it on the Internet.

I have nothing to do for the whole day. Smoke more meth. Smoke weed. Fuck, I hope I can get drunk tonight. I need relief. Time to masturbate. I don't want to, but I have to. I can't get it up because the voices are loud.

I would do it and feel filthy. The meth would be seeping out of my pores, my eyes would be dark, and my pupils would be enlarged from the meth and from shutting my eyes so hard while jerking off. I would be sore down there for a few days. Despite the soreness, I might even do it a few more times. I felt so out of control.

You'll always be alone because you've jerked off too much on meth. Every time you do it, the psychosis gets worse. Self-esteem gets taken down a peg. You'll always be crazy. You'll always have flashbacks to these voices and these feelings because you're too much of a pussy to speak for yourself. You <u>have to</u> drink and medicate because your psychosis is so strong. You're fucked. You're unsaveable!

"Nate......" No response. "NATE! What are you doing, boy? You okay?" A friend would ask with genuine concern.

Sometimes I wouldn't even answer. I would be mad that he even asked. I thought he had to know how bad it was.

Sarcastic cunt knows I'm fucked up. Is he being sarcastic?

I can imagine how weird it would have looked when they would ask me how I was doing and I wouldn't answer, or I would shake my head in irritation and give some off-the-wall response about how I thought they could hear what I just thought to myself. Being crazy is the loneliest place to be. My brain would listen partially to people's conversations while my voices ran rampant.

In psychosis, I would pick out certain phrases or words and rearrange the sentences in my head with selective hearing and use them to justify my insanity as if they were talking about me. I would rearrange words and misinterpret things as metaphors, or I thought there was always something snide or an underlying hint someone was telling me while I was having a conversation with them. I needed someone to talk to more than anything, but I couldn't trust a soul, because I couldn't handle even the simplest of conversations.

They're mind-fucking you with their words.

Early on in my drug use, I would be paranoid about others talking about me or thinking my friends were against me. But this was now bigger than that. This was no longer an insecurity in the back of my head. This was my brain on high alert at all times. Everyone is a threat, and no one can be trusted.

Cameras are everywhere. Your friends hate you, because they have to hate your other personalities in order to beat them out of you.

I would drink in the nights and get a small relief. I would talk a little bit and think I did something therapeutic for myself, and the next morning would be worse than the last. I felt it taking a toll on my body, too. My brain was like mush; I could almost feel the drugs putting holes on my brain. I experienced frequent hallucinations. Not just the shadow people. The shadow people had been on my mind for years, and they had now become normal. The walls would move and vibrate and that was normal too. This was something deeper and almost indescribable. It was my perception. It was how people would look at me and maybe even offer a smile or a joke, and I would perceive it as a threat. The hallucinations and voices made it impossible. I would be stuck in my head listening to my psycho-babble and maybe tune into another conversation temporarily. I recall someone talking about a serial killer or a murder on the news. My brain would rearrange the words, and I made a complicated rationale that made me believe they were talking about me. I convinced myself that I was capable of being a serial killer.

How bad is this sickness? How far will this take me over the edge? Does this mean I'm a psychopath now? Am I capable of murder or suicide now that I've gone over the edge?

Once I had the idea that I was insane in my head, a whole new world of toxic behaviors opened up. This was not a funny trip anymore. My boundaries and morals that I had grown up with were trashed. After all, this isn't Nate in control anymore. This is meth and psychosis. This was getting scary.

I had seen people like me before I lost control. The crazy tweakers.

I'll never be like them. I was raised right. I know how to do my dope.

But here it is, right in my face: the same psychosis I saw in all those lunatics I swore I would never be like. I was embarrassed every single day. Being a drug addict was low enough before. Now I was a drug addict who was insane—mentally ill. The embarrassment was turning me bitter. Not being able to talk, being ridiculed by my friends, telling myself I was too brain-damaged to communicate. I thought cameras were in my room. I thought I had a TV show of people in America watching me and laughing at my pain. I look back now and see this is almost comical. If it had lasted only a day or two on a bad meth bender, I could have laughed it off; but this lasted for a few years. Every day.

I celebrated my worst birthday in Ray's house. I turned 19. I remember waking up and seeing that they'd left me a bowl of meth unsmoked.

Just one bowl? They better buy me some beer.

I told myself I wouldn't go crazy today, but I finished the bowl and then went crazy. I did my best to do a few chores around the house and stay distracted from myself. Eventually, it caught up, and by the time everyone got home to celebrate, I was lost in a dark mental hole. So much for a good day. Not even on my birthday. I was alone downstairs and heard them call me upstairs to talk to me. I made it to the top of the stairs and all of my friends screamed "HAPPY BIRTHDAY" and showered me with silly string. Everyone was smiling and ecstatic. They thought they were so fucking clever. I didn't smile once. I don't even think I said anything. After they ran out of silly string, they started to notice my expressionless face. They all looked at me like I was crazy, and I suffocated their excitement quickly, so we could get back to smoking meth, and I could go back to my hole. Things seemed to take a turn for the worse after that birthday.

After a couple of days, or weeks, who knows, I smoked crack for my first time. My buddy Jay, his mom, and I were already loaded on meth, like normal, when the dealer came upstairs to see what we were doing. He got to talking and explained he had more coke, crack, meth, and some weed.

When he mentioned crack, my buddy Jay looked at his mom like a kid in a candy store and said "Mom! Did you hear that? He has some crack!" It was shocking to see the dynamics of this mother/son relationship. When we smoked it, I didn't even really get high. I was too lost in psychosis and had a huge tolerance from meth.

My first panic attack was at Ray's house a few weeks later. I was strung out, and I heard my friend Jay and Ray's girlfriend talk about someone who had cancer. The intensity of talking about someone they knew or cared about who had cancer had disrupted my meth trance, and now a part of me was listening to their conversation while trying to manage the voices in my head. I thought they were talking about me. Then I threw the idea around in my head. I started to rationalize it somehow. I convinced myself that from all the drugs I had done, and the stress, that I had given myself cancer. Everything slowed down. The voices went away.

I only heard one voice, and I felt a very distinct fear I'd never felt before. It didn't stop. I was powerless. It reminded me of how it felt when I took too big of a shot of meth. It comes for you and it doesn't stop. You go past the point of having fun and just want it to stop, but it keeps hitting you harder and harder.

I have cancer ... I have cancer ... I have cancer ...

After saying it over and over, it started to become real. The shock hit me. It literally shocked my brain and body. I felt it in my stomach first. It moved up from stomach, slowly crept into my chest, and then went into my head. Nausea. Then my throat seemed to close, and my breathing got harder. It came to my head. The panic keeps coming and coming. Impending doom, worsening and worsening by the second.

The feeling made it into my head and my vision started to get starry. Most of the stars were green and looked like a screen over my eyes. It set in my head and hurt. I couldn't talk. Then everything went black. My peripheral vision was completely blocked, and all I could see was the floor. It reminded me of when I was a child learning to swim. That feeling when you are sinking in the water and panicking. You start to inhale water. You feel like no one is going to help you and you're going to die. The relief that comes when your parents grab your hand and pull you back is so comforting. No one grabbed my hand this time. They didn't know anything was wrong. I sat in silence and blacked out, and no one would ever have known what I just went through.

Reject of Rejects

After a few months of listening to too much of my psychobabble, Ray kicked me out of his house. What a blessing. I was injecting multiple times a day and smoking more meth than I could handle. My negative attitude got me kicked out of my own circle for a while.

I was kicked out of the circle by a bunch of lowlifes for being lower than them, I thought.

The fear and paranoia turned into bitterness and malicious desires. Every time I tried to explain how much pain I was in, I was told "that's just a part of life," or "all of us are going through that." They were mistaken. This was different. Because of how timid and quiet I was, no one had any idea that I had started thinking of myself as a psychopath. I was hurt and unvalidated, a recipe for disaster. I blamed others for how I felt. I thought they were all plotting against me and trying to give me some sort of "treatment" for being insane. That's how I justified the hallucinations of them talking about me and "mind-fucking" me with their words. It started with me thinking close friends were messing with me, then it turned into hallucinations of gang stalking.

After getting kicked out of Ray's house, I moved back in with my parents. I took a week off from doing meth and blew through an ounce of weed by myself. I got sick too. My body had become dependent on meth, and I got sick without it. I went back to my old routine. Go out, get high, go crazy, get kicked out or become intolerant of insanity and come back home, broken. The psychosis never let up. The week off did nothing, and I thought I was screwed for life. So, I started giving up. I stopped fighting the insanity. I gave in and it almost killed me. Whenever a CD would skip, or a movie would skip, I would blame it on the gang-stalkers. Someone was messing with me. I gave in to the thoughts; I didn't think it was meth anymore. I was sure this was real.

Were mechanical birds with cameras in their eyeballs outside watching me? Sure, sounds reasonable.

After a bad bender, I came home in the middle of the day. No one was home. Just me and meth and psychosis. I hadn't gotten high in a while, but hadn't slept in two days. A CD skipped.

They don't want me to hear it. They're watching me and controlling me. Trying to make me stop being crazy with that secret treatment. Gang stalking. They can't control me. They're out to get me. The CD is skipping again. They're skipping it. If I cut myself, they have to stop because I am a danger to myself. Cutting my wrists isn't good enough anymore. They don't get the point. I'm going for the throat this time. I'm going to cut my fucking throat, you fuckers. I know you can hear this. You know what I'm about to do. You can hear my split personality talking. They're going to wish they didn't fuck with me. Here's the box cutter. Razor's out. SLIIIIIIIIIT!!!

All voices stopped. I snapped back to reality quick. I had just slit my own neck. I waited a second to see if this was real. Time stood still. I finally remembered who I was in an instant. I'm Nate Wilson, son of Julie and Wes, two loving parents. I used to play baseball and skateboard and go to church. I used to feel the love of God and others before I did drugs. I used to be sensitive and nice. I used to be empathetic. My friend Morgan always said I gave the biggest and best hugs. I haven't hugged like that since I died. Oh wait, I mean since she died.

A million thoughts in one second and then everything froze. I got up and rushed to the bathroom. I looked at my face, not the slit in my neck but my face. My eyes. What used to be big green and welcoming eyes were covered by huge black, dilated, strung-out pupils. They say your eyes are the window to your soul. And they're right, because mine are black as night. My eyelids were a shade of purple and oily. Expressionless face.

This body and brain is run by someone else. Meth? The devil? Brain damage? Demons? Trauma? All of the above.

This moment lasted what seemed like a lifetime. My neck lay open with revealed flesh and no blood for about a minute. As I stared at my face, red trickled down my neck. Panicked, I went to the medicine cabinet and grabbed gauze.

I didn't mean this. I didn't mean to do this. I'm sorry, God. I'm sorry mom and dad.

It was never supposed to get this bad. This all started as a party during homecoming week 3 years ago. I was supposed to be different. Now people are dead. Young people. Good people. Beautiful people.

I'm sorry. I'm sorry for showing the needle to my friends. I'm sorry for being alive. I'm sorry. I'm so sorry.

I don't want to die. I want to be better. I know tomorrow I won't want to be better, though. This feeling won't last. The only time I feel normal is when I feel guilty. My self-punishment to level out all the bad things I've done. It feels good to feel bad. All the other times are the evil, ruthless, and remorseless me. It's all I've known for . . . years now. I still think of myself as 15 or 16, but as I looked in the mirror, I realized I was supposed to be a young man. I was 19 now.

As I lay my head down, holding gauze over my neck, I prayed I wouldn't die. I didn't really want to die this time. Not like when I was ripping my forearm apart or when I had a gun in my mouth. And if I did want to die, I wouldn't want to bleed out and suffer. I've suffered enough in this life. After a few minutes, I figured out I wasn't going to die, and the remorse started to fade.

At least I'm worn out now; I've outrun psychosis for now. I know it will be back tomorrow. I know I'm going to crave meth tomorrow. I know tomorrow I will be alone again. But for now, I will enjoy the silence and feelings of remorse until it runs dry. And then I will sleep.

Jail

Sometime after getting kicked out of Ray's house, I awoke to the sheriff knocking on my parents' front door.

"Can you go put a shirt on, Mr. Wilson?"

This felt bad. The walk to my room was tense and uncomfortable. I had slept for a day or two, since my last binge and was sober rather quickly now. I still had psychosis and voices, but had a bit better reasoning. I didn't understand what was going on. I knew I was going to jail, but couldn't figure out why. I hadn't done anything but get high recently, and they had no probable cause for that. I came back down with a shirt on and stepped onto the front porch. I was told I was under arrest for giving false information to a pawn broker.

Now that rings a bell. What stolen property was it? There was so much stolen over the past year. Who knows? Who cares? So, this was it—my first time going to jail. My luck had run out this time; no more lost computer files and no more getting out of this. It was almost a relief, like I had finally got what I deserved, and I could now forgive myself a bit and let the courts take care of my guilty conscience. Part of me was relieved and the other half was in panic. I had never been to a jail, and I was scared.

My panic and the calm, swift, and routine movements of the cops were disturbing. My life was in total chaos and they couldn't care less. "Just doing my job," I'm certain was the cliché response that was in my head. I sat in booking, looking around everywhere and at everybody. Psychosis is on full throttle and everyone can hear my panic. I got tossed into the holding cell to await my jumpsuit and to find out where I'll be sleeping.

I heard two other inmates who had been there before talk and joke around. Every joke was about me, I was sure, and in spite of feeling antagonized, I could tell they were not a threat. One guy was talking about how he just wanted to get out and get needles and heroin, and the other just talked about drinking. I might have said a few words and maybe even mentioned that I inject drugs, too, but they paid no attention.

They probably think I am lying. I don't fit the profile of a hardened addict. I look normal. Like a college kid or something.

I took a nap for a few hours and awoke to a guard telling me to get ready to move into my cell. I grabbed my thin mattress and a crate and a baggie with a toothbrush, toothpaste, and a thin bar of soap. It felt heavy. I was weak from the lifestyle I had chosen to live. I couldn't show them that I was tired or weak, but I was. I walked into the pod with my heart racing. I was expecting everyone to be staring at me, which they were. In my mind, they had already seen me or heard of me as the crazy kid from Woodland Park.

They have seen you on camera. They have heard your thoughts. They hear you right now.

I walked up the stairs and made my way to the room. I saw my cellmate; his name was Brian. He was quick to introduce himself and seemed okay. He was not a drug addict, I could tell. He was a little too chipper and knew his intent. I didn't know what his intent was, though. We talked about each other's charges and talked about life. As soon as I brought up my drug use, he was quick to try to top my story. He boasted about doing cocaine and drinking. He'd snorted quarter ounces in one night by himself.

A combination of exaggerated stories and lack of street lingo told me he was lying. He was not crazy enough. I could tell by how he put his words together, by body language, and the stories about the rest of his life. They didn't match up. And I knew what a liar looked like; I was one too. Likely, he was doing it to make himself look badass in jail, to look like he could size up, but he wasn't fooling me.

As the days went by, he lied more, and I let him. I didn't have time to argue. Eventually, he came up with the story that he did cocaine in California with the hot girl from *Saved by the Bell*, when he used to be a "baller." I quit listening after that.

He was a jiu-jitsu master, too, and he beat people up at parties all the time. The truth was probably that he was a single guy, sheltered as a child, and rebelled a little too much as an adult because of it. He probably wound up a half-alcoholic and got a DUI, and he was likely as scared as I was of jail. But that's okay. God bless this man's life. I hope he never knows what it's like to be like me or live my life.

I spent five nights in the Teller County Jail. On the fifth day, I was moved to El Paso County Jail, or CJC, the jail for Colorado Springs. I thought I was headed for state prison. The El Paso County sheriffs didn't just handcuff me like the Teller County sheriff; they shackled my hands to my waist and used a long chain that ran to my feet to connect my wrist to my waist and my waist to my ankles. I started having a panic attack as they spun the chain around my waist. This was so unfamiliar and scary. I remember stepping into the back of the El Paso County van. A barrier was between the driver and passenger and the back of the van where convicts and suspects were seated.

There were five other guys, a few from other county jails and a few coming back from state prisons, for sentencing on other cases. Some of them were making small talk between themselves, and my psychosis played along with their conversation, thinking they could hear me out loud. I had been sober for a little over a week, and I still had to deal with the psychosis. There was one guy who was coming from state prison who seemed like the alpha of the convicts. He had a salt-and-pepper hair that was pulled back in a ponytail. He had a five o'clock shadow, which was salt-and-pepper colored, too. He smiled often. He was much older, and his comfortability told me he had spent most of his life in handcuffs and behind bars.

Before we departed, one of the sheriff's deputies asked, "You guys need anything back there?"

The alpha replied, "A loaded crack pipe and a six pack and couple of fat hookers would do the trick, fellas!"

I was sold. I liked this guy.

"What's your name, youngster?" he asked.

"I'm Nate," I replied timidly.

"Well Nate, I'm Dave. What are you in here for?" he asked openly.

I told him about my charges, and he opened up to me immediately. My rookie status was transparent from my age and my skittish body language, so he kind of took me under his wing. Another man, with a clean-cut goatee, stared straight ahead at the wall right next to me. Whenever I replied to any questions, he smiled at my modest responses. He could tell I was new, too. Dave talked shit and cracked jokes all the way to El Paso County Jail and did his best to figure me, the quiet kid, out. He had no idea, but I was like him, a hardcore drug addict.

We got to the jail and my panic attacks had subsided for the time being. Booking took forever, just like at the other jail. I sat in my misery, my mind eating itself in there. They put on the news channel. I sat and watched and went insane. Finally, they took me to the pods. I went to my bunk and went straight to sleep.

As I left for court the next morning, I saw Dave. He wished me luck in the arraignment and said I will probably get out on a personal recognizance (PR) bond, meaning that I will get one get-out-of jail-free card. The arraignments were held across the hall from my pod in the video courtroom. Unlike a regular courtroom, you see the judge through a camera, so they don't have to transport inmates. It was loud, and everyone was told again and again to keep quiet. Brad, an old acquaintance I recognized from the streets, was making a fuss over his pizza getting cold in the pods. The chatter turned to silence as soon as the video screen with the judge came on. Eventually, it was my turn to step up to the camera and face the judge. Sure enough, she let me out on a PR bond. I got to the pod and immediately called my mom to ask her to pick me up. I had been watching this commercial for Carl's Jr. all week and I knew what my first request for her would be.

She picked me up—rescued me again. There was always a strange silence in these moments. I'm thankful to be out of jail, but I'm still me. Still tons of undealt-with issues. We had a talk about my life and my choices. I want to change. "I will change," I told her. I knew I was lying. She probably knew too. I still wasn't ready.

We got home and I immediately raided the liquor cabinet. Chug, chug, chug on my father's Bacardi Gold. One or two shots and I felt nothing, just barely enough to take the edge off. I rushed to my room and looked for weed or crystal shards I may have spilled on the carpet over the past few months, but found nothing.

I'm fucking pathetic.

Time to go to bed.

Chapter 5

The Moment of Truth

No one is untouchable, no man is bulletproof.
We all must meet our moment of truth.
Gang Starr

I didn't quit drugs after jail. Nope, not even close. I made more trips to jail, too. I didn't quit drinking. I even went out and stole things from time to time. A few weeks went by, and I was sentenced to unsupervised probation and a deferred sentence, meaning it would be expunged from my record if I cooperated and completed all of my community service and a theft class. I had started to do community service; sometimes I went stoned. I tried not to go on meth, because I couldn't handle the voices and being in public. My drug use slowed down, and I could have passed for a normal 19-year-old kid who used drugs recreationally but still drank every day. That was pretty typical for my age group and peers, I thought.

I loved my liquor. God, did I love alcohol. I clutched my fingers around the bottle as tightly as I could with every chug I took. It seemed to nurture my sick brain. I tried to reenact those nights at Ray's house, when the alcohol would kill all the voices in my head like an exterminator. I'd felt fearless with the mixture of alcohol and meth at Ray's house. I did this every night. I didn't care about how it tasted; I loved the burn.

After my first few drinks or shots, I got pleasure out of feeling that burn in my gut, knowing that relief was just minutes away. The psychosis still prevailed, still kicked the shit out of me every day. It was more manageable, since I had now slowed down on the drugs. I used meth and cocaine about once a week or every two weeks. I stayed drunk and stoned every day though.

Maybe there were a few months when I used only once or twice during that month. Suicide was still on my mind. Every day, I thought of it. It was like a safety net. Like if things got bad again, I always had that way out. I craved death as much as I craved alcohol. I craved death more than sex or food. What a relief it would be to be dead. No climbing this mountain of recovery. Ha! As if I could call what I was doing "recovery." No more burden on my parents, no more burden on my friends. No more voices and addiction.

What a treat it would be for everybody for me to be dead. After the first few months, the pain will fade for my loved ones. And deep down, even though they might not admit it, they will be relieved I am gone.

Time to Fight

The battle had begun. An ultimatum. Make positive steps toward getting well or step backwards and fall down the cliff of self-destruction. So, I set out to do what I was supposed to do. I went through the motions of being "normal." I faked it every day. I was tired of my friends complaining about me being negative and tired of them constantly saying I wasn't crazy, when I knew damn well something was wrong. It was like no matter how hard I wanted to be insane and be a victim to schizophrenia, my family and my friends refused to let me. They were like my lighthouse when I got lost in the dark sea of disarray and pain. If it weren't for them, I'd be dead. I cursed them for this as much as I praised them. This phase was not easy. Even though I didn't stay clean every day, I still look at these days as the beginning stages of my recovery.

I ventured out into the world, trying to socialize and act like I was in my prime and happy, and I would fail miserably over and over again. I had more panic attacks, most of the time from smoking weed or drinking too much. Smoking weed wasn't legal yet, but it was becoming more socially acceptable. Nearly everyone I knew was smoking it. It relieved their anxiety and was a reason to be social. I missed those days, because they reminded me of high school and what it was like before meth and insanity.

One night, I was playing poker at a friend's house after Lee had picked me up. I had been drinking all day and was starting to come down. I felt dehydrated and burnt out. Just a few weeks out from the last time I did meth, my brain was still foggy. I tried to talk with Lee, but the psychosis came on strong when I was sobering up. A group of eight of us stood in my friend Trevor's kitchen. I watched everyone socialize and laugh. Everything was moving fast. A bowl of weed topped with hash came around, and I ripped it as hard as I could. As soon as I blew the smoke out, the fear hit me—the fear of what had happened a few months ago at Ray's house. I tried to keep up with everyone talking, but there were too many conversations going on.

Quick, quick, think of something to say. Participate. Be a person

The weed started to kick in, and my sight started to get choppy. Everything was moving faster, and my consciousness couldn't keep up. It looked like a fast slideshow or watching a movie through an old projector. It might have been fun if I hadn't been looking through the eyes of schizophrenia. The fear became stronger. I couldn't remember what I'd told myself, but I know I was fighting with myself. I was fighting the doom and the panic. The harder I fought, the worse it got. How I wished I could start over, start my life over. The minutes went by and no one seemed to notice. I needed someone to help me or talk to me, but they were far above and beyond me, like I was lost in a hole. I had a list of things in my head that I could say to get me out, but I didn't know what to say.

"So, how's work?" I could say.

"This is good hash."

"What are we doing after this?"

All these phrases went through my head like a marquee, but they moved too fast for me to choose which one. I almost spoke, but second-guessed myself. Each time, it's like a dagger in my brain.

Part of my head thought rationally and tried to slow down. I could hear two of me in my head. Sometimes there was a good voice and a bad voice, and it was obvious which was which. After I panicked, though, I didn't know which one was good. Everything was turning a shade of black this time, and the doom was getting worse than ever before. I couldn't talk; I was out of control. I shifted in my seat uncomfortably. My choice of words changed; I didn't have options anymore because my brain was in fight-or-flight mode again. My whole body was tense, and my toes curled in my shoes. My palms were cold and sweaty. Only these words scrolled through the marquee in my head now:

"Do you have a gun?"

Suicide was the last option to get me out of this panic attack. My head was down, and everything went black. My ears were ringing. Sharp but invisible pain. No one has stopped to notice me either. This was worse than my panic attack at Ray's house. After about 30 seconds of indescribable mental pain, I looked up. I looked around. Everything was foggy, but a different kind of fog—a dizzy, slow feeling instead of a sharp, uneasy feeling. I felt sick, but it was better than panic and anxiety.

Then I could talk again. Suddenly, I didn't have to force my words out like most of the other times either. I was back on a flow.

"Where's the bathroom?" I asked.

"Down the hall, to the left. You okay, dude?" She kind of chuckled. "You're really pale, like a little green."

"Yeah, I'm good," I turned, without making eye contact.

I went to the bathroom and threw cold water on my face. I glanced into the bathroom mirror, but just for an instant because I didn't want to see my pathetic face. I sat down in front of the TV. My buddy's wife brought me some water and tried to help me. I told her I was okay, even though it wasn't the truth. Everyone continued through the night, and no one had any clue that this was the worst thing I had ever been through. I went through it silently and unnoticed.

Crutches

Eventually, I got a job at a car wash, but consistently showed up half drunk from the night before. I got a girlfriend in the summer 2007. I have no idea how, considering the confused state I was constantly in. Maybe because she was as drunk as I was, I suppose. Coming from the same town, I guess maybe she understood how things could spiral out of control, with all the tragedy and loss we had endured. I think she empathized with that. She put up with my drunken and drug-induced psycho-babble nonsense and did her best to relate. We stayed up nights after the partying and tried to talk about things. I think about one half of what I said and one half of what I heard might have made sense. The drinking was constant, and the drugs were on a gradual increase. I hid them from her, because I knew she hated all of it, but I ruined this relationship when she discovered I was still using cocaine and meth.

I still did my best to rely on alcohol to keep weaning myself off of drugs, but it was starting not to work. I had spent months and months trying to chase the same balanced high I had gotten at Ray's house, when I had just the right amount of meth in my system and just the right amount of alcohol to make me feel normal. New Year's Eve 2006 came to mind. Sitting there that night with a case of beer and an unlimited amount of meth, I drove as much of both substances into my body as I could until I passed out at about 4 a.m. It was like balancing on a tight rope. When I fell, demons were below, waiting to grab me and hold me down in the flames and eat my soul. The memory of my first panic attack lingered in the back of my head at all times.

The more I drank, the more distant I got from being content. What happened? I could always rely on alcohol to save me, and now it didn't have the same effect. I had been using alcohol since I was 14 years old to help numb out the world and make myself bolder, but it was backfiring. I wasn't the same smooth and cool drunk I used to be. I was sloppy, and my conversations were shallow and boring and uninteresting. I could see myself acting stupid and couldn't do anything about it. And I didn't have the wherewithal to sober up either.

My friends did their best to support me when I wasn't high on meth. They saw my struggle and stuck around despite my still-declining mental health. I stayed over at Lee's house often. We would play poker and watch On Demand movies and listen to music and drink. I still felt like the outcast and felt like a charity case.

How could anyone want to be around me?

I had nothing to offer and everything to ask for. I was building myself back up from nothing. I had no personality anymore from the drugs. I never had fun unless I was drunk, and I never let anyone hear my thoughts. I still felt like I was stupid, or brain-damaged and insane. Everyone else was getting laid and smiling and joking and laughing, making new good memories and meeting new people, giving the world a chance. I thought most people at 19 felt on top of the world and in their prime. I felt like I had already seen too much in this lifetime, and I wanted to be done with this life.

I was always in the background, silent, hurt, feeling unsaveable. What shocked me most was that people didn't seem to see this. Or they looked beyond it. I wanted to lull around in my own sorrow, and everyone around me was so resilient. A lot of them did the same drugs I did; they'd lost the same people I had. Why couldn't I recover? I tried constantly to explain my pain, but my friends wouldn't hear it. I think maybe they looked beyond the negativity I projected. They believed in me more than I believed in myself. They would call me out and tell me that I was wrong. It was harsh at first. It hurt to know that I was being a big baby, but it may have saved my life. I hope they know this. Despite their efforts, my mind was stuck in hell.

Homicidal Tendencies

Another night of drinking and playing poker at Lee's house. There were girls over, and as usual I drank myself into a silent stupor. Shot after shot, I couldn't quit. Everyone else was drinking and laughing and seemed to be elevating. I was drinking myself lower and lower. My thoughts became rampant. The panic started to set in. Who knows what started it? I might just have misunderstood someone and thought they were talking about me, and now that small window let all my demons come flooding in. It's so fucking scary when this happens. Impending doom, worsening and worsening by the second. The feeling of blood leaving my head reminded me of my first panic attack. It cycled from there; every negative thought affected me physically. Every thought felt like a dagger in my mind. I could feel the alcohol forcing its way back up. My mouth starts to water, and I know I'm about to puke.

No, it's okay. You're okay. Just act like everything is okay. Your mind will overcome this.

Reality says: "Too late. You should have thought positive thoughts earlier. You should have participated in the fun; you should have listened to your friends. You shouldn't take their advice for granted. You should have paid more attention to your friends than to alcohol."

Here it comes. Can't move. Too drunk. Can't make it to the toilet.

Puke everywhere. The girls, my friends, everyone looked at me and laughed. I felt like a freak. The girls say "EWWWW!!!" The smell is pungent, and there're chunks in my nose and in my teeth. I felt the acid burn at my teeth. My stomach burned and begged for nutrition. I tried to vomit into the cup nearest to me. About a quarter of it went into the cup; the rest went onto the carpet and my clothes. I heard comments start about how bad the smell was.

"What the fuck did you eat, bro?" Everyone giggles.

I was singled out now. I had felt like a freak in the back of my mind, and now that thought had become reality. The girls left, more than likely because of me. My friends were pissed, but they thought it was funny. I did my best to help clean, but I was drunk and useless. After we finished cleaning, I lay on the couch and tried to pass out. I felt a marker on my face. I opened my eyes and saw my two best friends giggling and telling me to hold still.

"Fuck you, man!" I said and swatted the marker away. "I just need sleep. Leave me alone, please," I begged them.

Please, not tonight, guys. I'm fucked up, I know. But this is not the night.

I tried to tell them.

If they only knew what this was like for me. This wasn't drinking with friends. This was trying to outrun psychosis for me. Running from myself. I didn't drink to have fun. I drank to kill myself and to kill my thoughts. This isn't fun for me. I tried to fall asleep again after I thought I had fought them off. As soon as I dozed off, I felt a marker on my ear.

"Fucking quit, guys!!!" I begged again.

They don't know how bad this is right now. I have to calm my anxiety before I can be cool. I'm not cool yet.

I moved to Lee's bed. Then they tried other torture tactics, like duct taping me. I thought I deserved this, but I wasn't accepting it. I've done this to others in the past, so this was karma. I moved to the spare bedroom, and after a few minutes, they barged in and tried to get me. I wrestled them off, and they laughed at my anger and frustration. I suppose this was their retaliation for all the nights they had to put up with my negative attitude and had walked in circles with me in lunacy, while I got my mind right. But this was the wrong night. They went outside to smoke a cigarette, and I finally got relief. But I'm done pleading. I went to the kitchen and grabbed a knife, about 9 inches long with a serrated edge and two points on the end. I moved to the couch and hid the knife under the blanket.

This is for every time they didn't believe I was crazy or that my insanity wasn't real. This is for every time they thought my insecurities were a joke. This is for being smarter and having their shit together. This is for not believing me. This is for the harassment I've endured from all my friends. You will now find out that I am crazy. This is for thinking I didn't have it as rough as you did in my perfect little Christian home. This is for me. First one to fuck with me is getting this to the gut. I'm ripping it right out and getting my other friend immediately after. Right in the fucking gut. This is the rock bottom. I'm ready to murder two of my best friends for fuckin' with me.

They entered the house as soon as they were done smoking cigarettes. I clutched the knife under my blanket and waited for one of them to approach me. This was the night I was done joking. They sat down on the couch and flipped the channels for a second. I cursed them more in my head—thinking they could hear me, thinking I was talking aloud. They stopped. They hadn't seen me grab the knife; I made sure of that. I wanted a reason to do something stupid like this. To prove to everyone that I **was** really crazy and psychotic. They didn't see me grab the knife, they weren't scared or intimidated. They just stopped messing with me at the right time. Divine intervention? I saw Lee go to his bed and go to sleep, and then Tim and I watched TV. I think we may have even had a friendly conversation about something while I clutched a knife under my blanket. I was ready to gut him a second ago, but now we were talking about life and back to being best friends. He had no idea. He never will. He passed out. I turned off the TV and put the knife away. I'd barely survived another night. And so did they.

Did I stop drinking? No. Did I stop doing drugs? Still no. I did accept a possibility that maybe I wasn't broadcasting my thoughts out loud. Maybe I had just done too much meth and created a delusion in my mind. I was about ready to kill two of my friends. Even though I thought people could tell what I was thinking, they didn't seem to care. But they were about to get stabbed.

What about all those other coincidences? I don't have a split personality. That's ludicrous anyway. I don't have any idea how the idea became engineered in my head. But sometimes, when I was on meth, I would be thinking something and the exact word I was thinking of, or situation, would be spoken about on the radio or by my friends.

Did this just happen too many times? I was obviously too far under the influence to understand and process it. I knew drugs were powerful, but this was insanity. I believed I qualified as mentally ill; I was insane. A crazy person. This is what schizophrenia looks like...a functioning schizophrenic.

Everyone else but me seemed to be in denial about it. Every time I tried to talk to someone about it, they told me to just forget it or block it out. Or, it's not me, it's just my head. Or it's just the drugs. "You're fine, Nate," they would always say. How annoying that was to me. They had no clue, and to prove my point I almost stabbed my two best friends in a moment of weakness and bitterness.

Slow Progress

Believe it or not, I was actually making some progress. I was starting to talk more and trying to open up about what was going on in my head. I can't say I opened up about my feelings or emotions, though. I didn't have any. I remember feeling pain and that's it. I was detached from my own mind and my own body. I could only describe what I was thinking objectively, as if I was looking in on another person's thoughts.

I rarely smiled. I was merely along for the ride. Eventually, the car wash went out of business, and I found a job painting houses with a family friend from church. His wife ran the first drug therapy program that I'd attended years earlier. I think he also empathized with my situation. Looking back, I don't think I was actually very good at painting houses, but I tried. I fought hard to do things to keep my mind occupied with something other than drugs and psychological havoc. I learned to socialize day by day. Starting conversations with new people was hard; I had no trust in them. If they weren't a drug addict, I believed they wouldn't ever relate to me or what I had been through. It was like I was learning to talk again, learning to talk after coming out of a drug-induced coma.

During summer 2007, I hung around Lee and some of my close friends who hadn't shut me out of their lives or weren't yet annoyed with my insane perspectives. Recovery was actually beginning. It started with talking to Lee. I told him everything. I knew that several years before, he had hit a bottom no one could understand, when he was drinking and driving and his girlfriend Sarah Jane had fallen off the top of the car while car surfing and died. I knew he could understand what it's like to self-hate, what it's like to feel outcast and singled out. I spent as much time as I could with him. His advice was so simple, yet spoke to me on a deep level that no one else could. I told him about being numb all the time and feeling nothing but pain.

"Well, you have to act sometimes," he said. "You have to fake the smile just to get through the moment and to humor people," he explained.

The "Fake it 'til you Make it" concept. Brilliant words these were. Fake it until you make it. That advice helped me survive for years, but it wasn't easy. This is why so many addicts fail. Faking life is painful. Faking a smile every day. That's what I started to do at every party I went to and got too drunk. Every time I made a mistake, I would smile and laugh instead of showing my self-hatred or getting down. Every time my friends picked on me for being a little off, I smiled through the fog. I started faking it, and my mind started to believe it. I found very small moments in which I was a little entertained or happy, moments I wasn't thinking about drugs, moments when I could feel vulnerable and be comfortable with it. I started getting out and doing things, like going camping again. I would go to parties with the kids I went to school with who were a few years younger than me. I felt like a freak compared to them, but I still showed up. Back in those days, going camping and chugging liquor and beer, and driving from party to party, wasn't as dangerous as what I could have been doing.

Unfortunately, the law didn't care that drinking and driving was actually a step down from some of the other things I could have been doing. I was busted for my first DUI in 2007. My buddy in the back had to vomit while I was driving us from our campsite to another party, so I pulled off the road as quickly as I could, with screeching tires and an abrupt turn of the wheel . . . right across the street from the sheriff's office. The cops said they heard the tires squeal and decided to come investigate. When they saw a kid outside vomiting and his friends around him laughing, they knew they'd hit the jackpot. It was a short ride to jail that night.

I spent three days in jail before I got released. I can't remember, but I think I was bailed out by my parents. They said since I had a job and I was trying, they would help me out. All in all, I sort of lucked out again: the district attorney was willing to keep my felony on a deferred sentence. So, I had to complete all my alcohol classes and more community service, and I would still get my felony expunged. I went through the painful DUI process. I would show up to classes every week, even if I was a little stoned, or hadn't slept in a night from coke or meth use. Even at that, my drug use was slowing down. I was using maybe only once or twice a month. I was learning how to function on drugs again, which was both good and bad—bad in that it enabled me to keep using, but good because I could keep a job, and it showed me that functioning on drugs was more work than it was worth. I was accepting the fact that it may be easier to be clean.

The weather was getting better and the house-painting business began to increase. Exactly what I needed. I met some others who were in similar situations of being on parole or probation, having an addiction issue, but still trying to get by. I finished the next two months painting and staying busy. Staying out of trouble too. I went about two months without getting high on meth at all. My brain chemistry was balancing out; my psychosis was still there, but manageable.

Since construction work is seasonal, when October came, my job came to a screeching halt. I called my boss one week in the middle of October, and he said, "I have one more house for ya, but after this, if you do have a job, it won't be working for me."

As the work slowed down, idle time became common in my days. Idle time means trouble for most drug addicts. My drug use increased and my money decreased. I tried a few times to get different jobs, with virtually no experience in anything except washing dishes, washing cars, and painting. I thought I had an opportunity to get a job with someone who had steady painting work on a military base, but because I was on probation I was not allowed to enter the base. The owner of the business was very friendly over the phone during the interview process, but once he heard I had been in trouble, and what for, he chimed in "Maybe next time you'll think twice about stealing!" Nope. I went back to what I knew: selling drugs and stealing.

November came and I spent time with my family on Thanksgiving. I still wasn't using drugs often and felt that I had quality time with them. I had a conversation with my cousin about the new PlayStation coming out. He gave me all the details on how badass it was, and I listened contentedly with no paranoia. I saw his kids and ate big. I made it sound as though I was doing well, because I had finally maintained a job for a few months and had made an honest buck.

I felt normal for the first time in a while. I thought I was medicating myself properly with the drugs. I wasn't using too much, but I was still able to numb my pain and my past.

The lie of addiction creeps in ever so slowly, and even though it's lied to me before, like when I was 16, it was creeping up on me again. It had evolved and grown because I had grown too. I had grown strong, but so, equally, had my addiction. They say that every year you are clean and get stronger, your addiction is in the corner doing pushups to keep up with you.

About three or four days after Thanksgiving, I had rounded up some money to buy beer, so I sat at home drinking. I was content. A buddy called me from the car wash, asking if I knew where to get some crystal meth. It sounded like a good night to do crystal. I had him pick me and another friend up, and we left for Colorado Springs. I only had a few beers in me and I was craving more of something. Anything. I couldn't have just a small buzz; I had to go all the way or nothing at all.

We pulled in to the hotel and I got the word from my dealer to wait in the parking lot, which was unusually full for winter. My friend got out to smoke and started walking around. I sat in the car with Jeremy and waited patiently for the drugs. Jeremy was older than me, and a nice guy, too. He didn't belong in this game. He had told me his story before. When he was in high school, he'd tried meth out to be cool or to join in the party, and it had gradually turned into an addiction. He was so out of place in the drug world, not malicious or selfish at all. He still lived with his parents, who were overprotective like mine used to be.

He would never be quite "right" in my eyes. He still looked like the same high schooler that became a victim to meth. From his mannerisms and behaviors, I read that he thought it may have been his parents' fault. They sheltered him and tried to keep him a sweet little kid into his high school years, and then he rebelled as a reaction. His parents tried to teach him to be confident in himself as long as he walked the straight and narrow, but never taught him to rise up from devastating life events. Jeremy was probably forced to go to church, like I was, and hated himself for not being the perfect kid that he was supposed to be. His parents loved him, but probably didn't encourage him much now that he'd been tainted by drugs. His parents were not educated about recovery—and why he acted the way he did.

He tried to compensate for being a drug addict by being passive or extra nice. He was trying to balance what his parents had taught him and what they had never prepared him for. He couldn't open up to them because they were judgmental and would show disapproval or lecture him about what he already knew. He needed to know he was significant, had value—that God didn't hate him because he would get high. His parents' approval wasn't needed anymore, even though he still longed for it out of guilt. They no longer knew the way to his success like he had thought in his childhood. His glory years weren't behind him yet and he still has potential, even though his parents might not see it.

Someone needed to tell him these things, someone he looked up to. He needed to believe he was loveable. He needed to hear it, but it wouldn't be from me. On the contrary, I was going to use this against him as a means to keep us both high. I would get him drugs and feed his pain with meth. He would go through me to get the drugs, and we would both lull in our manic-depressive heads. I was preying on his sadness, and because he was not selfish meant that he couldn't think like me. He didn't know what I was doing to him or, if he did, he didn't have enough confidence or self-respect to stop it.

I'm a fuckin' snake.

The door opened and my buddy Cayden had copper wire in his hand. Cayden was more like me. He knew the game and knew you had to be all about yourself and your drugs to survive and thrive.

"Look what I found, buddy," he smirked as he jumped into the back seat.

"Is there more?" I asked with excitement.

"Yep, but I need your help," he said, as he reached for the door handle.

Installment Plan

Before I even agreed, he knew I was down to steal something and make a quick dollar. We bolted out the car doors and he led me to the Qwest telephone company's work truck. We started unloading all the copper and aluminum, but before we could get everything out, a man approached us.

"What the hell are you kids doing?" he demanded.

"Well, my buddy works for Qwest and told us we could have this copper," I lied.

"Actually, this is my employee's truck and I know for a fact he didn't tell you guys that. I'm calling the cops," he said.

We ran to the car and took off. We stopped at the nearest gas station to lay low. I went inside to use the bathroom and to walk off my adrenaline rush. I came back outside and just as I approached the car door, the police pulled up and blocked us in. Instantly, I felt like an idiot.

Why didn't we hit the interstate? You know Jeremy would have done anything we told him to.

They didn't ask any questions. They just put us in cuffs and took us to booking. This was my second time in 9 months at CJC, and the third arrest in a year. I wasn't sure how bad my criminal charge was yet. I sat in booking forever. It was about 11 p.m. as I watched a news channel with no volume.

Wait! I see Jeremy's car on the TV, with police lighting up the gas station parking lot. Looks like we made the news. No, I'm not impressed. I've done bigger shit than this—must have been a boring night for news. All we did was steal copper. This is just a PR gimmick to make it look like cops are all over catching every little crime that transpires in the city.

This fed my psychosis a little, the part of me that thinks people are constantly watching me. I can't say that it was really under control, but I was learning to ignore it, or rather to keep my feelings out of what goes on in my head. Thus, I had no feelings most of the time. It didn't always work. In fact, most of the time, it didn't work. When I did too much meth or stayed up too long, I relapsed into old thinking and psychosis. But I was learning to cope with being an insane person. Facing my insanity was too uncomfortable to deal with. And as long as I was an active addict I would not step out of my comfort zone.

In booking, there was a friend's brother who knew Jeremy. He called him "Jumanji" and teased him a bit. It was funny to me. This time I could hear the jokes, unlike my last lock up. It wasn't as scary this time. I was used to thinking people were out to get me, so this tense type of atmosphere seemed normal. I knew I wouldn't get raped. If I flew under the radar, I'd be fine. We were escorted to general population and to bed I went.

I spent 2 weeks in jail this time, my longest stay yet. After a few days, I went to court and they read my charges...criminal trespass, some type of theft, and some type of criminal mischief or something. I didn't really know anything about it, except that it was another felony. My probation officer told me that my deferred sentence was being revoked, so this meant that I would have two felony convictions.

The powerlessness of my situation made me care even less. I should have been concerned. Or I should have wanted to make a change, but I knew deep down I wouldn't. I contemplated it, but didn't have any great epiphany as to what I could do to stay clean and straighten out. I guess I felt like I had cut back enough on my drug use...and felt I didn't have any more compromise left in me.

After a few weeks, my old roommate from rehab was put into the same jail pod. We ate at chow and kicked it together, along with our friend POG (Prince Of the Ghetto). Jail was more fun this time. Not fun, but better than the first time. Your brain's natural defense is to make the most of a bad time. POG was always telling stories about being a pimp and smoking crack. He was about 6' 4", big and black, and talked with gangster slang. He was funny as hell too. We played cards, made jokes about jail rape, and told stories about our crazy lives.

I still felt misplaced, though, like I didn't belong there. I felt like I saw something others didn't see, I just didn't know what to make of it yet. We talked about getting clean, or at least just smoking weed and drinking when we got out. In my bay, there were six bunks and 12 beds.

I liked most everyone there, except the one kid who looked like Jesus. He reminded me of the first time I was locked up in the Teller County jail with another kid who looked like Jesus. I called him kid—even though I was only a year older—because he was fascinated to be in jail. He lipped off just enough to be annoying, but he somehow dodged getting his ass kicked by a Nazi in the pod. He ran his mouth and acted like a know-it-all, commenting on everything. It was apparent that he was there by accident; he didn't belong. He'd made some small mistake and ended up in here. He hadn't done many drugs or crime. He'd maybe just pushed the boundaries, like he did with his mouth. I couldn't stand him. Every time I was locked up, there was some young kid who thought jail life was cool, and I couldn't stand it. If only they knew. Maybe this one knew he would never be in here again and that was why he didn't care.

And maybe the thought, belief, fear, and truth that I will be back in lock up again is what pisses me off. Maybe it's not him at all.

Making Bail for Christmas

About a week before Christmas, my parents bailed me out. Bless their big hearts. I stayed clean for about three days, then I smoked weed with my buddy Ryan while we wrapped his Christmas presents. He was an addict like me, but wasn't living the same lifestyle. He lived in the mountains, snowboarded, and had fun with his drugs—transparently happier than I was. He did his drugs and partied, but maintained a job, a life, and a girlfriend.

His strength amazed me. I didn't know how to be like that. I didn't know how to do drugs without it involving crime. I didn't know how to love, and I was still haunted by what meth had done to me sexually. I thought I had things going for me with my painting job, and then the work ran out. I felt like—wondered whether—God had cursed me. For not being there for my friends when they died? For taking for granted what my life could have been?

The holidays passed, along with more court dates, and more drugs and alcohol. The oppression of having an open case was dissolving my heart. My boss called and said more work was on the horizon. I was attending DUI classes, and I had a probation officer I would talk with once a month. She was on a work visa from England. It annoyed me that she was from another country telling me what to do in a town where I had lived my whole life. I would show up to DUI classes stoned, sometimes strung out from the night before. Never too far gone, though, I stayed functional for fear of catching another case.

Learning

As the cold winter came to an end, the brightness of spring enshrouded me with hope and brought forward new perspectives. I was willing to do some work on myself. If you are truly wanting to stay sober, it's inevitable that you are going to grow, like it or not. I laid off of meth and cocaine when spring started. I was willing to give my life a chance. Day after day, I chased that frame of mind I had before drugs. That clarity. That peace. I mostly ignored the voices in my head. I'd had a conversation with my mom in the winter about how to deal with my schizophrenic mentality. After seeing a psychiatrist for a few weeks and making broken attempts at staying clean or healing, I took her advice to just ignore the voices.

"Just like Russell Crowe does in *A Beautiful Mind*," she said.

So, I locked it away. I gave up on trying to explain or comprehend it. Years of thinking I was being watched on TV, thinking my thoughts were being broadcast, thinking people were harassing me...I just shoved in the closet. The delusion of cameras being in my house and in my car left first. The thought broadcasting stayed in my mind, but I ignored it.

The painting business picked up and I had reason to stay busy and out of trouble. Work hours were plentiful. As expected, I kept on with my drinking and occasional weed. I had fun with it, though. Every day became an adventure in staying off meth and learning about who I was. Even on a bad day, it was better than a good day on meth. It seemed I was coming out of my hole. I reconnected with some of the "normal" childhood friends I had grown up with who were back from college for the summer. We would go party sometimes or just hang out and watch movies. I had my first summer fling with a girl. After years of being numb and too paranoid to talk to anyone, I found the two of us watching comedy and talking about life. I had the chance with her to open up about those past few years and how crazy they were.

I didn't sound that jaded when I talked to her. I seemed sane, like all my reactions to what had happened in my crazy life were reasonable, considering the amount of pain I'd had to endure. I had a clear mind and was able to communicate easily and seamlessly, with no paranoia or second guessing. She sat and listened, giving me feedback. I had no idea what it meant to her or whether she had this with other guys back at college, but I didn't care. It was enough for me to be satisfied in the moment.

We spent more nights together hanging out and going to dinner, watching movies, kicking it with friends. I worked hard during the day and unloaded at night. I even started to cut back a bit on drinking. I tried to keep it to the weekends. Summer 2008 was a blast.

I hadn't thought about being crazy in a long time, like in psychosis, which I still was. The voices would run rampant sometimes, but I knew it was complete and utter bullshit. It was drugs. It was the drug addiction still trying to keep me chained.

You can't have my soul anymore. I will persevere. I will withstand these trials.

I had many friends and our bond was strong. I felt that I was a part of the group again. My friends respected me for staying clean and keeping my drug use down, and for holding a job and not being depressed and such a crazy person all the time. I was able to connect with them again. The summer was coming to its end, and work was slowing down again. I found myself with more and more idle time, and it was getting comfortable. I was starting to have whole weeks off with nothing to do. I still had money left from working all summer and had recently bought a car from my buddy, Lee.

The Ford Probe. This car had seen a lot of miles and a lot of memories. Passed down through a lot of friends to end up with me. It was an honor to drive that hunk of garbage. It smelled like gas or oil or some other unidentifiable fumes. The tires were down to the wires. But I loved it. This was the first car I'd bought by myself. I spent these days transitioning into the fall by driving around with friends, smoking weed, and drinking in the night.

It had been 6 months since I'd done meth. I even quit smoking cigarettes for about a month. Slower and slower, the days would go by and curiosity was increasing. Some younger kids were calling me for a cocaine connection and knew of someone I had met while painting houses. I used this as leverage to create for myself a part-time position selling "blow." It was too easy not to do that. It's what I was used to. This was more comfortable than having a job. I didn't like doing coke anymore, either, which made it easier to sell. I would just as soon shoot meth than deal with a comedown on coke.

I had made a connection with one of the Mexicans through work and landed myself a drug-dealing gangster connection. He always had coke and weed. He was in the gun-dealing business, too. He showed me all his guns and made sure I knew he could get a napalm gun as well. I was scoring from him one night and I told him that these guys I was dealing to were pressuring me for the drugs a little too hard. He told me he had no problem going outside and shooting them all if I needed. I told him I could handle it. I liked this guy.

It's a curious thing how this unfolded. I invited one little vice back into my life, and all of a sudden the life I thought I'd left was in my face again. I saw it happening day by day and did nothing to stop it. I wasn't even in denial that anything bad was going to happen. It was just all I had known.

Heroin

A close friend had tried heroin for the first time and said he'd found his new drug of choice. I knew the second he told me about it that I was going to try it. I had barely cracked the door by selling coke again and now the demons came rushing in to swirl around my head.

I pictured myself on a sidewalk on an overcast day:

> The leaves have turned on the trees, and the wind blows the falling leaves over the sidewalks and all around me as I step-by-step down the sidewalk. I'm in a neighborhood right outside of downtown and all of the houses are fancy, but old, Victorian style, large and grand. They are old enough to be haunted, and the darkness of each house makes them appear as such. As the wind ensues, the demons follow. They float like the wind and are nearly transparent. They are a dark grey and swirl around my head. They move too fast for my mind to comprehend their faces.
>
> I'm trying to avoid them, block them out, and walk in peace, so I keep my head down and increase my stride. At first, I'm sure I can ignore them because I feel strong. I haven't had a confrontation with demons in so long. But they don't stop. More arise, because they smell my fear. I ignore them for a few blocks, but their quick and startling motions and their whispers are starting to get to me. I see people walking past me giving me weird looks. They can't see my demons; they see only my flinches and feel my tension.

I look back and see my family and friends who love me. I see all the work I've put into my sobriety. I see my childhood. I see myself as a happy person. I am reminded of who I am deep down. As I start to feel strong again, a demon steps into my line of vision. *No time for looking back. Time waits for no man.*

I turn around and step onward. Now I flinch when the demons speak into my ear. One whisper becomes five. Five becomes ten, and now the voices are constant. My whole body is tense, and my steps become slower. Each time I set my foot down I tremble. My ankle rolls, and I almost fall over. The wind is increasing, and now demons and leaves swirl in the whirlwinds around me like little tornadoes of chaos.

Some of the demons laugh, while the others whisper. They laugh harder as soon as they see a tear. Now a weakness is exposed. Now they know I am breakable. Now I'm sobbing. All the work I've put in up to this point is on trial, and the devil is my judge. I can feel him and his demons critique everything I do. From the way I walk to the way I think to the way I cry. I don't see God because I refuse to look up. I'm hanging by a thread now, and mentally I have given up. I am taking each step with almost no faith. There is no more purpose in my walk, and I can't see what's ahead. It's darker now, and I can't see. There are no humans anymore, just the demons and the darkness.

My tears are pouring, and the whispers are louder now. The demons mock me in every way. I can hear the demons talk about everything I've done wrong. I can hear them blame me for Xaq and Morgan. They blame me for my friends' meth addictions. They blame me for making my parents' lives miserable. They tell me I'm not worthy of having love. They tell me I was never loved anyway. There's a crack in the sidewalk that I can't see. I catch it with my toe and fall forward. I try to put my hands out in front of myself to catch my fall, but I'm too slow. The demons are all laughing and cackling hysterically now. Right before my face hits the sidewalk, I clench my eyes shut and brace for impact.

I opened my eyes, and I was poking my arm with a syringe. The needle was sharp and pleasant. It slid into my skin smoothly and lingered in the vein painlessly, waiting for me to inject. The needle was so smooth it reminded me of the worst needle I had ever used. It was bent like a banana and had been used so many times that the fluid measurement numbers on the barrel of the syringe were all worn off.

The liquid in my needle wasn't a murky white with meth anymore. It was brown. It looked like mud. I pulled back and watched the blood spill into the needle. Dark blood and the brown mixture made the needle look like it was full of black liquid.

I hesitated, then I plunged with uncertainty into my vein. I pulled it out and instantly felt warmth coming over my body. The taste ran through my tongue. A dull, toxic taste. Nasty. It started in my heart and came over my head. Then it moved out into my limbs, out to every appendage, right down to my tiniest toe.

This was different from the meth and moved me in the opposite direction. Down, down, down, down. Lower and lower. It suppressed my heart rate, and my thoughts came to a halt. My head felt feverish, but without the pain. The euphoria was warm and welcoming. It came on slowly but unwavering. I looked up and saw my friends laughing at me. They almost brought me back to reality.

I was shaking as I rinsed my needle. I stuck the dirty point into the water and pulled back the clean water and squirted the bloody and brown liquid into the carpet. My hands were moving slowly and felt like they weighed a thousand pounds. My body was moving slowly. Everything was moving slowly.

We went outside to smoke a cigarette. Each step I took was miscalculated and misaligned, like being drunk times a thousand, worse than being the drunkest I had ever been. We smoked cigarettes and I tried to talk. My words were slurred and slow. My stomach was bubbling with anger. It burned with each inhalation of tobacco smoke. I put my cigarette out and stumbled into the bathroom. Each slow stiff step felt like I was walking on pins and needles. Each step shocked my head and rattled my skull.

I made it to the bathroom and vomited my breakfast burrito and green tea. It didn't hurt like it should. It didn't burn like it should. The vomit came out so smoothly and without a fight from my body. My gag reflex was asleep. I puked, and then everything was down, down, down again. Now it's back to being high.

We hopped into the car and drove to my house with plans to play music. I had played drums for a few years and had a natural talent for it. Once when I was high on meth in Guitar Center, I had a lady come up to me and ask if I gave lessons when I was practicing. Apparently, I still sounded polished even high on meth. I declined because I was too preoccupied with my addiction and had little ambition.

In the back seat of the car, I laid my head down while my friends were talking to me from the front. I heard them, but I was far behind them in a world far, far away. This felt like speaking through a wormhole from another dimension. They asked me if I was okay and I said yes. I heard them laughing some more and singing, "Nate did too much! Nate did too much!" They were still laughing. I gave a little giggle when I could muster the energy. I was in the most comfortable zone I'd ever been in.

We made it to my house. I went to the bathroom and puked again—six times in about one hour. I slowly came back from another dimension, but a part of me was still way behind. We made a few attempts at playing music, but couldn't find the tempo. I was too high to keep tempo on the drums. But the nausea stopped.

We decided to go back to the Springs to see Lee, and to shoot more drugs at his house. It was nice and mellow when we walked in; the lights were low and the TV was on. No loud noises, no partying or belligerence. We cooked up some more shots and shot them into our veins again. The feeling was instant, but less abrupt than before. The nausea came back within minutes and we all took turns puking in Lee's toilet. We spent the night watching TV, nodding off, and puking. Lee didn't use drugs; he just watched us for entertainment.

I woke up the next morning and chalked off the previous day to just another life experience. Another drug in the books. I went about a month before I did heroin again. The business in painting houses had slowed almost completely and just like the year before, my idle time increased. I was now a part-time painter and part-time heroin user and coke dealer. Sometimes I would still use meth, because it could help offset the comedown with heroin.

Using heroin gradually became an everyday thing, and it was beginning to make me sick when I didn't have any. I worked a whole day with my nose sniffling, and by the end of the day I felt body aches. My coworker was cracking jokes, asking me if I was on cocaine.

Nope, but close.

By the time Halloween rolled around, I was on heroin full time. My last day painting was on Halloween. I went to the house of a friend who had been saving me a shot for when I got off of work. Our other friend, who rarely used drugs, was over. He gave me the needle, and I rolled up my sleeve. I injected with ease, pulled out, and carried on like nothing was happening.

"Jesus....." he shook his head in disbelief.

I realized how numb I was to this style. I'd forgotten that injecting drugs was hardcore. I forgot it was toxic. I was desensitized. It was simply my life. I was going to die this way. I was slowly starting to mess up my probation, too. I forgot to do my community service and was sent to jail for three days. I shot up heroin 20 minutes before I turned myself in. I remember nodding off and drooling during booking. When I was released, within just a few hours I was dealing and snorting coke and drinking. I still did coke occasionally, even though I didn't like it. Most of the time I would medicate the cocaine comedown with heroin and inject speed balls, meaning I would inject cocaine and heroin at the same time. We also did "trainwrecks", which was meth, cocaine, and heroin. This was right around the holidays, and the girl I had my summer fling with was back to visit. I had plans to hang out with her as soon as I got out of jail. Instead, I blew her off and sold and snorted coke the whole night and got wasted. I woke up the next morning and cried in the shower.

It's getting bad again. The drugs are in charge now.

I texted her and apologized. She was so patient. She saw something in me others didn't see. She knew me before drugs and she knew me after. She understood. As an addict, I took her for granted, not knowing what I had. I told myself she would be gone soon and back in college anyway. She would meet some guy who was better than me. More mature, more money. NOT ADDICTED TO HEROIN!

My friends were on the same page as I was, conditioned for drugs and the lifestyle it brought. We spent a lot of time at Lee's house. He used to just watch us do drugs. He never stood up to us or kicked us out, he just tolerated our drug use. But it started to wear on him, the "partying" and having fun. We teased each other for being so high and being so out of it. Then Lee got curious, wondering what the hype was about and why we kept doing it. Then he tried it. And we had no problem sharing it.

Misery loves company. Within a short time, Lee was using as much as we were.

Heroin Addicted

Work painting houses had now officially gone out of season, and the drug game was on in full force. I was depressed one day and happily ignorant the next. Managing my psychosis on drugs and going to probation meetings and my DUI classes was like walking a tight rope. I showed up plenty of times to my DUI classes high on heroin or meth or whatever. I even talked and participated. I went to my probation meetings. On one occasion, I went in sick and sweaty from heroin withdrawal. I sat uncomfortably for 20 minutes before I got out and hit the ground running in search of smack. Discomfort from the withdrawal was amplified by 100 from the anxiety of how bad I was messing up. As soon as I would come down on one drug, I was high on another.

I used meth, cocaine, and heroin together for the first time, and then I drank to come down. It was like a never-ending party. More and more numbing. I didn't go crazy this time. I lied to myself that I had beaten my mental illness, when really it was just stuffed in the back of my brain. I knew my psychosis could burst out of me at any moment, especially under the influence. The voices still ran rampant, but I had grown to realize everything I told myself was a lie. I had two people inside of me. Sometimes I would listen and let them beat me down and tell me what a shit I was. The fight just wore me down some days.

After a hard bender and a few nights of speed balling, I finally crashed at my friend Jay's house after I drank myself to sleep. The first part of the bender was heroin. I injected heroin at least five to six times a day for two months, until the dealer moved back to Mexico for fear of getting busted. I went through my first withdrawal. It lasted a few days, but I medicated with meth and beer. I spent two days injecting and smoking meth and drinking. Then on the fourth day, I scored a large amount of cocaine for a friend and nursed my comedown from meth and heroin with drinking beer and injecting cocaine.

I literally felt like I was killing myself in the most painless way. It was perfect for me and my little death wish until the next day when I woke up in a haze. A nasty film was in my mouth from smoking so many cigarettes and all the meth and whatever else my body was processing. Fuck, this hurts! My body ached. My joints were stiff. My nose was clogged like I was sick, and I couldn't smell anything. I forced pizza into my stomach, even though I wasn't hungry. I was shaky from low blood sugar—a combination of alcohol withdrawal and having no nutrients in my system—and being just flat out beat up.

There's no life in me. I've wasted all my soul on drugs. Nothing left to give anyone. No intellect. No love. Nothing interesting or profound. Nothing new.

I spent the first half of the day trying to recover. I took a shower and started to wake up.

My phone rang. It was Lee, asking for cocaine. I told him I'd call him back. I didn't want to. I didn't want to AT ALL. I knew Lee was unstable. I was at his house about two and half months ago, when I was clean, because he was suicidal and said he needed me there. He was always there for me when I was sad. I remember, in the depths of my dark psychosis, reading a text from him that said, "Don't do anything to hurt yourself, Nate. It would fuck me up so bad." That meant a lot to me. This was when I felt like all my friends had abandoned me for all my struggles with psychosis. Everyone was tired of listening to me except for Lee.

So, here I sat, phone in hand. Lee wanted coke. I knew better. I looked up at Jay. "Lee doesn't need this," I told him. "He's too unstable."

"Do what you feel is right," Jay said.

I sat in silence.

I called up the dealer to make sure I was clear to make a buy, and then I called Lee and told him I'm on the way. I got Lee's bag, and then, as always, I got my bag for being a valued customer. My dealer told me I was the lead cocaine buyer. Not the first time I've been told this. I've been known to make my dealer's rich, but I was always too much of a drug fiend to maintain my own wealth in money. I did all the drugs instead of make money. I took my bags to Lee's house and was ready to get high. There were certain vibes in the room; everyone was happy about the drugs except Lee.

"I've been fucking up, Lee," I told him.

"Well, that's on you, dude." He was irritated. He had no more advice for me. He didn't want to talk with me. This was the first time he sounded angry with me, like he just wanted to do the drugs and get it over with.

He snorted his lines, and I did my first shot. It hit hard, but it wasn't enough. My tolerance was high after the binge. I loaded up another, but I couldn't find my vein. I put the needle in time after time, but it wouldn't hit.

I was shaking like a leaf. I kept the needle in and moved it around, hoping I could find a vein. My veins were shot at this point. It was disturbing to watch the needle twist around in my arm. It's a nervous thing to watch—the point might break off in my desperate-junkie's skin at any moment. Finally, the blood spilled back into the needle. I plunged the drugs as quickly as possible. The rush hit. Then it hit again.

It wasn't stopping; it hit harder. And harder. I sat on the couch.

Wait, no! Here comes the vomit.

I was blacked out, but I made my way outside to puke. It was painful. Everything was sharp. My body had been through too much. My heart was loud and pounding against my chest, like it was angry. Puking turned into dry heaving and more pain, sharp little stabs in my stomach and in my brain. Finally, the vomit stopped and I sucked in for oxygen. I shook with every breath. Everything was bright and starry, shocking and sharp. I could hear others talking. Their words felt sharp, even sharper when I put together what they were saying. Bright and sharp and fast. Everything was fast. I took some breaths. For minutes. I'm not sure how long I stood on the porch, catching my breath.

Okay. Okay. Get a grip.

I took slow, stuttering steps back inside and sat down. I tried to have a conversation with someone to keep the fear in my mind at bay. After 45 minutes, I started to come down, but my body was still shaken. I made Jay drive because I couldn't stop shaking. We got back to his house and I ate more pizza to try to level out. It took about eight beers before I felt normal. This was the second time cocaine almost got me.

I think I stayed clean for about three days after Lee's house. I crashed and slept for days. In the meantime, Lee had broken up with his girlfriend. I talked with her, and a conversation came up about a night when Lee had hit on my girlfriend Shanna, one night as a joke, when we were partying. Lee's girlfriend confronted him about it, and now Lee was mad at me for telling her. It seemed his life was falling away slowly. He called and told me he wanted to fight me.

"I won't fuck you up too bad," he said.

This broke my heart. My older brother turning on me. Someone whose approval I had always sought out had just shunned me. I ignored him and decided to let him cool off. He would have beat my ass all strung out like this anyway. I continued doing heroin. This time harder. I kept dealing coke to keep the money rolling in for my smack habit. I had recently connected with a neighbor who'd moved here from California. His name was Nick. He was Mexican and a [10]sureno gang member, and he did a lot of heroin. The odds of a California gang member who shot more smack than I did living in our small town were slim to none, but, sure enough, he moved in right next to my parents' house. We teamed up: He would pay for the drugs and I would be the ride, driving around in my beat-up Probe, scoring drugs, pulling up to red lights and then shooting up and driving off or pulling up to stoplights and vomiting out the side of my car. I risked our lives, driving up the winding Ute Pass from Colorado Springs to Woodland Park, nodding off from the heroin.

A kick in the teeth

After a few weeks, I decided I needed to detox. I didn't want to pay for detox, so I decided my grandma's house would do. She could nurse me while I was sick. I did my last shot that morning and went to her house and waited for withdrawals. Then I got a call from my top cocaine customer, who wanted a big bag of coke, and I was ready to get it for him. It was getting dark, and my withdrawals were not setting in yet. I saw my phone ringing. It was Lee. I picked it up. He was crying, sobbing, broken. I asked him what was wrong, but I couldn't understand what he was saying. I tried to ask him yes or no questions to distinguish what was wrong.

"Are you sad about your girlfriend?" I asked.

"Yeah, yeah," he said in between sobs.

I asked him what I could do to help. "I don't know, I don't know," he said over and over. I tried to talk him down, but he didn't seem to be calming down.

"I'm going to go now," he said reluctantly.

---

[10] Surenos came from southern California in 1967. Surenos are groups of loosely affiliated gangs that give tribute to Mexican mafia, especially in U.S. correctional facilities.

I could tell he didn't want to go. He wanted to tell me something more, and I didn't know what it was. I didn't know how to help. I could either go sell cocaine or be there for my friend. What does a heroin addict do? Nate would go to his friend's house and stay awake until his friend went to sleep to make sure he's okay. He would talk with him about anything, and open up and relate, because he knows his friend's life could be at stake.

I didn't know where Nate was that night, but he wasn't around. Just a selfish heroin addict. All Lee had to do was tell me he wanted me over there and I would have been there, but my drug-riddled brain couldn't comprehend the right decision. I texted him and said, "I can be there for you." And then I left to go do my cocaine deal. I completed the deal, I made my money, and made it back to Grandma's safely. I pulled into the driveway and my phone was ringing. It was my buddy John.

"What's up, bro?"

"Nate. Lee hanged himself and he is now dead," he said.

"No. No............ No!"

No. No. No. I just talked to him.

Denial. Of course, denial comes first. I could watch myself go through the stages of denial like watching another person. Part of me was detached and lost from reality, and the other part of me was still human. The part that is hurting and in distress. I'd just talked to him an hour ago, and my brain wasn't going to comprehend this. I'd been through this before. It was like fucking clockwork now. Denial, anger, bargaining, depression, and then acceptance.

This was different from any other death. I was older and more aware. Despite the heroin, I felt this death more. I wasn't naïve like when Xaq and Morgan and Travis died. It hurt more. Even in being a numb drug addict, I still thought I was out of the woods for some reason. Of course, I cried, but I felt like my tears didn't mean shit anymore. There's no amount of grieving that will bring someone back, and I resented that. This resentment was why I chose not to grieve. I chose to be numb again. I choose not to feel anything. I chose drugs.

I wanted to sit in my Grandma's driveway and hide from the whole world, but I couldn't do that. The only way I was facing the world was by staying high. So, I did. The thought of detoxing went out the window when Lee died. I knew my cycle too well. I didn't even have a choice at that point; I had to get high. It's all I knew.

What else was I going to do? Get therapy? Tell my probation officer? Ha! I knew her response before I even heard it. "Well, Nate this is just a part of life," she would say. Or "Be careful what friends you choose." Then she would discourage me from going down the wrong path. HAHA!! Some cliché emotionally detached response that doesn't show empathy, because if she felt something for me she might understand why I am such a fucked-up drug addict, and she wouldn't preach at me for being in trouble all the time. She would understand that drug addicts are really just hurt people. She would understand that the only reason we choose to rebel is because their stupid system isn't set up to help our problems, but just to mold us into an obedient and shallow human being who does what they want us to, or it's designed to keep us sick and addicted and trapped in the system and it doesn't work!!

> *Ahhhh, here's the anger part of grief, the part where I feel like no one understands. Every time someone tells me they're sorry, it means nothing, because I know this pain inside of me is so deep that they can't possibly sympathize or empathize. I know this all too well. This is where, belligerently and intentionally, I emotionally isolate myself so I can do drugs and not have a conscience.*

I couldn't show my pain anymore. It was buried under years of substance abuse, death after death, abandonment from friends, and self-hatred. I didn't know how to show my sadness. And then there's the psychosis, like a blocked road in my head. Every time I tried to cry, the voices increased, and I couldn't even concentrate on what I felt. I wondered how long it would take to deal with any of these problems. How many years of therapy or me sitting in an empty field trying to meditate, trying to wrap my head around all the pain and loss I've gone through and trying to come up with a sound and reasonable and peaceful new philosophy on why my life ended up like this? Well, that wasn't happening. This wasn't a movie. This was my life. My harsh life. It was time to get high.

I stayed up, high on meth, for two nights. My heroin withdrawal actually wasn't as bad as I'd expected. Maybe because I was in so much emotional turbulence, I didn't have time to get dope sick. I got a call on the second night; I was asked to speak at Lee's funeral. So, I sat down with a bottle in my room, by myself, and outlined a eulogy. I wasn't clean, so it felt vain, but then again, everything I did was vain.

I spoke at the funeral. I faked it at the reception. Then I did heroin afterward with a few friends. I heard a loud noise on my back porch that I thought nothing of, and I went to take a shower. When I came back out, my buddy Ryan had fallen over. His lips were blue. I shook his body, then shook his head. Overdose. I sat him up, woke him up, and started pouring water on his head. He gradually opened his eyes and started slurring his words. We took him over to Mexican Nick's house, because Nick was the heroin guru. He said he would help us with Ryan, if we gave him some heroin.

This life! It was like the harsh moments never ended. It was like we were born with a curse. A month after Lee hanged himself, another Woodland Park friend, Molly, died in a drinking and driving accident. I couldn't count how many friends had died. Not just acquaintances, but people whom I had loved, people who had changed my life. I knew there would probably be more. Would I be next? I knew I deserved it, and that I also craved it.

Numb

There was never a dull moment, and our crazy stories were never-ending. We took one tiny little step off the wrong edge and fell into an undertow of addiction. These instances of friends dying, and hanging around gangsters, and participating in my first robbery used to be crazy; it used to be shocking. But they became everyday occurrences. I thrived on the negative. I thrived in pain and chaos, just like Christopher Walken said in *Suicide Kings*:

> "And it always starts with the first . . . bet or babe or snort, fix, whatever, until it becomes easy, and after that, you don't feel nothing."

Desensitized. Numb. We had become so traumatized that we didn't understand the chaos we lived in. In fact, we laughed at some of the things that used to frighten us—like making fun of my friend the next day for chattering his teeth, when he was falling asleep after a near overdose on heroin. We mocked a single mother who shoved a container full of fake urine inside of her to take a urinalysis, so she wouldn't lose her kid, overlooking how tragic it was for her and for her kid to grow up with a strung-out mother. I made fun of my jail experiences or suicide attempts to make myself sound like I was just being a funny type of crazy or just being stupid. Anything to avoid the truth that I was actually severely damaged inside, hurt and scared.

I just wanted to be someone else my whole life. I wanted to be the opposite of who my parents had raised me to be, which was a successful, functioning member of society. I was supposed to go to college, graduate, and get married. Something easy. Nothing risky. I was supposed to be my parents' potboiler story to tell at small get-togethers when friends asked the courteous question, "How is your son doing?" I couldn't figure out why I resented that so much, why I questioned everything they taught me.

I first felt antisocial around my freshmen year of high school, thinking about society as a twisted cult of judgmental, unoriginal thinkers—like a herd of cows being led to a slaughterhouse, and the slaughterhouse as a metaphor for their boring-ass lives. Get a job, get bitched at for the rest of your life by a woman you used to love, and then vent about it during bowling league or softball games, like every other pathetic robot in the United States.

I saw the world as a machine built to keep the elitists rich and snobby at the cost of our sweat and pain. I didn't want to be successful. I wanted to be a rebel. I wanted to start a rebellion. This is what was so appealing about the underground addict lifestyle—a separate society that the rest of the world seemed to be blind to, the very thing my parents tried to shelter me from. In this sub-society, there would be no order, only chaos. Everything in reverse. We would get off on the things that we shouldn't, steal, fight. We would indulge in our flaws, instead of hiding or denying them like the rest of the world. We would hide during the day and stay awake at night, and, we would explicitly expose the world to what happens to people who are rejected, oppressed, and not loved.

I loved being an outcast, because it gave me an excuse to rebel. The power behind my middle finger pointed at society and at the world was intoxicating, as much as the drug. I thought of our crew as a rebel resistance against the evil empire. What a shame that we were blinded by drugs. All that wasted energy spent in hating or resisting, instead of getting behind an actual cause. This was a lack of opportunity. Tragedy. Nothing to lose. It was how I felt, and I reacted accordingly.

Breaking Point

I was at a party, drinking a few beers. I knew I had to drive, so I drank only five or six. I had a stash of Xanax pills in my car, and I was ready to take those. I knew that they're strong, so I was going to wait until I was at a friend's house and didn't have to drive. My friend told me he needed a ride to his house, so he could get to work in the morning. I told him I had to pick up a friend, and then we could go. We hopped into the car and cruised. I was a little tipsy, but in control. I had driven drunk so many times now. I didn't have my license back from my first DUI, but I still drove.

I made it to Monica's house, then we headed to Woodland Park from Colorado Springs, laughing, sipping on a beer, and talking. It was about a 30-minute drive. I was anxious to get pills into my system, since I hadn't had smack in a few days. I took two pills about 15 minutes into the drive, assuming they would kick in by the time I got to my destination.

We had reached Woodland Park. My hometown. Where all the heartache was born. The road was getting twisty and harder to follow, but I wasn't worried because we were almost there. Then the lights in my rearview mirror caught my attention, flashing and trying to alert my foggy brain. I knew what was happening, but I wasn't as panicked as I should have been. Somewhere deep down, I knew there was trouble, but I couldn't feel it. I pulled over and waited for the officer to make it to my window.

"Sir, can I see your license and registration, and can you step out of the vehicle?" he asked. He talked fast and smoothly. He was on his game, and I was not.

Be smoooooth, Nate. Smoooooth. Be quick and calculating with your movements.

My brain was not connected to my body. I opened the door and I could barely move my legs. They were so distant from me. The ground was like a thousand-foot step down for me. I walked toward the back of the car.

"Walk ten feet down in a line, heel over toe, and then come back," he instructed. I walked down the line. It took forever, and I couldn't see the ground. For some reason, I grasped onto the hope that I might have done okay.

"Now what?" I slurred.

"Now you come back like instructed, sir," he said patiently.

I walked back. He asked more questions that puzzled me. I tried to be cool. He instructed me to breathe into the breathalyzer. Then I was sitting in my car again. I don't know how. Things got foggier as the pills kicked in harder. I watched them open up my glove compartment and ask me about the dirty syringes. I think I tried to say they were for my diabetic father.

I was put in the back of the cop car, handcuffed.

Piss. I have to piss.

The cop was talking to my friends, taking forever. It's painful now. My body was trying to detox the pills and the beer. I somehow managed to pull my pants down just slightly and started letting the tension from my bladder go into the opposite side of the cop car. I had relieved myself in the back of a car only once before, stuck in a traffic jam in Denver, coming back from a backpacking trip when I was 15. That was a better time in life. I pulled my pants up and sat back in the seat.

Finally, the car was moving, and I went in and out of conscious thought. Another DUI suspect was arrested and sat next to me in my piss.

The cop buckled him in and asked, "What'd you piss yourself, man?" I shrugged my shoulders, hiding a smile.

We moved to the holding cell in the city jail. I don't remember how I got in there. It was cold and I was agitated. I tried to lie down and sleep, but it was too cold. I shivered and wrapped my shirt around my legs, like I used to in grade school. I shivered for a few minutes, before I started banging on the door and asking for a blanket. Banging and banging and no answer.

Is this the fucking drunk tank? I'm not drunk enough to need detox. This is an insult.

Banging and banging and yelling. Yelling nonsense. I grabbed the toilet paper from the cold, stainless steel toilet. I threw it as hard as I could at the camera in the ceiling. Yelling and now throwing the toilet paper. I had no concept of time or how long I was screaming for. Eventually, I laid down and passed out. I woke up in a different holding cell in Teller County Jail. I knew this cell better. I had been here before. I was a little less hazy now. I looked at the clock. It was past midnight. It was quiet. I thought it was Tuesday or Wednesday.

I'm in jail again. I'm on probation. I'm on felony probation. I'm more than likely going to be sent to prison. I'm too small to be sent to prison. I can't handle prison.

The gravity of my situation set in. That panicked feeling came that I was waiting for. The smell of county jail set in as well, a very plain smell, a stale smell. It wasn't a nasty smell, but it was very unwelcoming to me. Everything was concrete and cold. Prince of the Ghetto had told me just a year earlier that they kept it cold because it kept the sex drive down, and inmates wouldn't try to fuck each other. I was still high, but sensible.

I can't handle these consequences. I can't handle this life.

I watched the activity throughout the booking area. There were only a couple officers on duty. I watched how often they passed the window. Time passed: 15 minutes, maybe 30. Or maybe it was 45 minutes. I don't know, but it was more than 15. There was a telephone in the holding cell . . . to tell loved ones you're in trouble, and that they need to bail you out. The phone sat low to the ground and the cord made a loop. It looked like it would fit nicely around my neck. I sat on the ground. The cord was about 4 inches above my chin. Perfect. Perfect for me to hang myself.

I used my hands to push off the ground and elevate my head into the loop. The officer had just finished with his last round, and I knew he wouldn't be coming around for a little while—enough time for me to die. Enough time for me to cut off the oxygen to my brain and not be revived.

The second I lowered my neck on the cord, I felt pain and pressure. My tongue started to force itself out of my mouth. I tried to hold still, but it hurt so bad with 150 pounds of pressure on my neck. I squirmed and couldn't take the pain. I lifted myself off. This wasn't sad, like other suicide attempts. There were no tears. I was too numb from the Xanax to feel sad. It was more like a mission that I needed to accomplish as objectively as possible. It just made more sense than trying to live as a drunk and drug addict; more sense than jail or prison, or more heartbreak, or whatever else God or life wants to throw my way. I caught my breath and lifted my head back through the loop again. Sharp pain. I can't stand sharp pain.

Endure. Endure. Keep pushing. Everything will go black soon. Two minutes to pass out.

The gaps in the cord pinched my neck. Squirming and gagging and spitting. Not even past 30 seconds. It was just too painful. I lifted myself off the loop. Come to find out, I put the cord too low on my neck. I was angry, pissed at the cord for pinching me, mad at the stupid cops and my Probation officer. But most off all, I was angry with myself. I hated myself. I hated myself for not knowing when to quit. I hated myself for being a cop magnet. I hated myself for continuing to use despite the consequences. I hated myself for not being able to stop when I should. I wished I was normal, like the girl I had the summer fling with. I would have given anything to have her life, to have control, to go back in time and change who I was. I didn't know where I would start. Would I change the moment I did meth? Would I change the moment I did coke? Heroin? When I started stealing in third grade? My babysitter? Where did the road take a turn for the worse? It was all so cluttered, I couldn't even make sense of it.

I fell asleep and awoke to a jail guard bringing me breakfast. I was still hazy because of how strong the Xanax was. I took naps throughout the day, until they moved me to general population. I made friends quicker and easier than before. Felt like a second home. I wasn't shocked by who was there. There were the white guys, who were typically locals from our small community. Then there were always no more than five black guys, who were being transferred to and from federal or state prisons. About 15 to 20 Mexicans were being deported.

I hung with the white guys, because I was white and they were local. I usually have mutual friends or I am already friends with them. But I shared a cell with a Mexican, who was obnoxious and obviously undereducated. He was the cliché fuck-up of society. Born without a chance. His whole family was in a gang, and he had been since he was 12, he told me. He smoked and sold meth and gang-banged. His jokes had no wit and he laughed like a loud asshole. But in his own way, he was funny and somewhat pitiable.

He told me he was being transferred through the Federal Prison system because he was on a reservation when he got busted with meth in South Dakota. He had some interesting stories. His brother had been shot in the cheek and survived. He got his nephews stoned when they were 10 years old. He had no remorse for any of his crimes; they were not his fault. He had no idea what doing right was.

In the cell next to us was another Mexican who had been down for 20 years, and he was doing jailhouse tattoos. He hollowed out a pencil and stuck a sharpened staple where the lead would be and tied thread around it from his socks to keep it intact. He sharpened the staple by rapidly scribbling it on the stainless steel faucet or toilet. He crushed the lead and poured it into a cap from the toothpaste tube. Then he took the shampoo and mixed it with the crushed lead and made it into ink. To get the outline of the tattoo onto the skin he drew a design on a napkin, then rubbed the clear deodorant on the area where the tattoo would go on someone's skin. He placed the napkin on top of the spot pasted with deodorant. The pencil outline from the napkin stuck to the skin, and then he had his design.

I was captivated, and I knew I would be there for at least a couple days, so I agreed to let my cellmate tattoo me. Just a small design on my wrist, in case he messed it up. It read "Dizzle," my nickname from high school, given to me by my friends. I don't know why I was given this name, but I missed it, and I wanted it on me for no good reason other than it will be a good laugh. This would be my second tattoo, in addition to the one for Xaq on my back. The tattoo took about six hours, even though it was only four inches long and one inch high. It gave us an activity at night when we couldn't sleep.

We told each other stories about drugs, women, fights, and what we were going to do when we got out. Every story was nearly the same. Everyone was going to quit doing smack or meth or crack and just stick to drinking and smoking and selling weed when they got out of prison or jail. Some of my friends visited, which made a world of difference to me. They were friends who had been through the same things I had. They understood why I was in there, and they didn't judge me or look down on me. They took pictures and we had laughs.

I played basketball against all the deportees, who looked like they had never played before in their lives. I beat them, and it reminded me of my childhood, playing sports and being competitive. I hadn't felt competitive in years, because I was always too high to play or compete in anything. I quit skateboarding because I knew I couldn't do what I used to. I didn't do anything that involved running, because I was a smoker and always in a calorie deficit and had no energy. In jail, I was eating plenty, working out, and recovering physically. I didn't think much about the night I tried to commit suicide. It had happened so many times before, and could very well happen again.

2nd Annual Ruining of Christmas

I sat in jail for about two weeks, until Christmas Eve arrived. The whole time I had been begging my parents to bail me out as a Christmas present. Just as I got put as trustee so I could get "good time," I saw the guard point at me through the glass in his office. He pointed at me and waved bye, which meant I was going home.

My parents caved again, an addict's dream come true. I already knew I was going to get drunk. Maybe I'd have to wait until after Christmas, but that was all I thought of. My parents knew it, too. I think we were all happy, as long as it wasn't drugs, and I wasn't driving. I made it through Christmas Day, then went to a friend's house on Christmas night. It was his birthday, and he asked me if I could make it an extra "white" Christmas. Cocaine. Of course, I would. I loved selling cocaine, and I already figured I was headed for prison, after violating my felony probation. Nothing to lose.

The day after I was bailed, I made the cocaine deal for a close friend, and I got wasted that night. Lee's sister met up with us. We picked her up from a bar. She was with her friends, drowning the pain of her brother's death. They were all attractive and classy looking. Then there was us. She was smiling and laughing with her friends. I felt bad for picking her up, but she did call on us. I felt bad for her. I felt like we were the harsh reality and smack in the face. She got in the car and we all exchanged hugs. We talked for only a few minutes before she started bawling. Here it was, the painful truth. The injection of pain into her heart. We reminded her of Lee. For me, she was the closest I'd get to seeing Lee again, and for her, we were the closest she would get to seeing him again.

Reckoning

The following week, I had to meet with my probation officer to talk about my revocation. I walked into the office and saw a Hispanic male with a hard and straightened face sitting behind the desk. He was firm, and he didn't move a muscle. He barely looked me in the eye. When he did, he made it brief and made it look like it took extra effort to even see eye to eye. My current probation officer was standing behind him with her arms crossed.

"Have a seat, Nate. I am Nick Herrera," he said assertively.

I sat down and the shaming and cliché questions began. What happened? Why was I hanging out with people who were drinking? How long had this been going on? Am I using other substances? Nick gave me his personal philosophy, too,

"I HATE people who drink and drive. I have lost many friends to it," he declared.

A part of me laughed. I don't know this man's story, but I can tell he has no idea how many friends I've lost. Strange thing was, I hated people who drank and drove, too. I hated myself for my lack of control. I know it killed Sarah Jane; I know it killed Morgan and Molly and hundreds of thousands of others I didn't know, around the world. And then they dropped the bomb.

"So this will be revoked and turned into a DOC case. How does that make you feel?" I paused and fear hit me. My face turned pale and emotionless.

"DOC case?" I said with fake disbelief.

"Yes, you've run out of chances, Nate," Nick said with a thick Hispanic accent.

Behind tears of desperation, I said "I will kill myself before I go to prison."

There was a pause, and I saw the shock in their eyes. I liked that. I felt like I had control again; I could always fall back on suicide. It was like my rock. When things got tough, I could choose to opt out. It was comforting to me.

"Well, we may have some options. We just need to speak to the D.A," Nick replied.

To end the session, they finished with lecturing me on not drinking until my court date. I faked all the right answers well. I didn't argue, and I didn't give away the truth—the truth that I couldn't stop, and that I was psychologically damaged. I wished they could see my progress, how I could control my psychosis better and the voices in my head. I wished they could see that I don't steal anymore. Nope. I was still scum, though, shooting heroin as often as my budget would allow and selling cocaine to college kids.

There was no justifying this. I am a drug addict and alcoholic, and a hurt person who can't stop.

I left that meeting feeling low, where I thought I belonged. I had gone months, maybe even more than a year thinking I was a great person and an exceptional functioning addict, and now I had been humbled. My plan was to spend the rest of my life getting high and drunk and numbing out the pain.

Why won't the world just let me be? Why can't I just deal with my sickness how I want? Why do people care about me? I don't want them to. I don't want two loving parents. I don't want friends that care enough to give me deep emotion-filled talks on why I should get clean and quit trying to kill myself. I want to get high for a while, and if I die that's okay. I don't care whether I die. It would be a blessing.

There are too many who care, though. After Xaq, Lee, Morgan, Sarah Jane, and all the others who died before them, I can't do it. I'd be even more of a shit bag than I am already, and I wouldn't be around to fix it this time. Maybe getting better wasn't such a bad idea, but now I was probably headed to prison, and I don't care.

I spent months waiting for my sentencing. Court date to court date was how I lived. Drinking as much as I could. It felt wrong the first few weeks out of jail, because I was back to the habit. I used meth three times despite being on UAs. I would use meth the day after my UA, knowing I had a week to clear my urine. I passed all UAs. I waited. I existed. I didn't thrive, I didn't think I would thrive. I merely breathed. I woke up, faked looking for a job, drank in the night, did it again. I was a nobody. I was hollow, trying to fill myself with liquor and sometimes meth and cigarettes and fake smiles. When I looked at anything, I saw darkness. I saw happy people as fake people. I called myself a realist, though I was, in fact, a masochist and pessimist.

I had no dreams; I hadn't in years. I always thought I would be a part of some rebellion that ended the world or that I would die. As time progressed and I did not, my court date came. It landed on the Monday of my 21st birthday. I was to be convicted and sentenced for my second DUI and two felonies before I was 21. And even that wasn't as bad as it could have been.

The proceedings were nothing unusual. They talked their fancy law lingo, and I nodded my head and said yes. The sentence was given: only 20 days in county jail and a lot of community service, DUI classes, therapy, and supervised probation. The same requirements I couldn't get done before, only in greater quantity.

"Mr. Wilson, you are not to drink on your probation this time. Last time, you didn't do so well," said the judge, who was my basketball coach when I was in 6th grade.

No drinking on a 21st birthday after you just sentenced me to three years of anxiety.

Jailhouse Reflections

I spent two days binge drinking, and then the next three days loaded up on heroin. I enjoyed the week, actually. Friday came, and 7 o'clock was nearing. My fun was ending. My life was changing. I didn't know it yet though. I took my hit I had been waiting for, then turned myself in. I had been in here before, nodding off and drooling on myself. I waited for the cops to give me my jumpsuit and blanket and all my toiletries. I walked mindlessly to my cell. It was about midnight, and my cellmate was sleeping. I could see tan skin and the letters LA tattooed on the back of his head.

I put my thin mattress on the bunk, stashed all my toiletries away, and I climbed into bed and stared at the dimmed fluorescent light. It had a layer of dust across it. It looked dirty, and I could smell that familiar smell of an institution. Smelled like concrete.

I felt plastic, like a robot—like I'd become the one thing I swore I would never let society make me become. I had no personality. Any personality traits I had I faked. I learned them from other people I wanted to be like. People who I thought were better than me. Or tougher. Or more gangster. More respected. Whatever. I just didn't want to be me. I didn't know who I was.

I had spent a few years trying to rebuild myself, but I had been doing it in the wrong direction. Ever since that day at the hospital and at detox, I had been trying to grow up. Learning to fake everything on drugs wasn't supposed to happen. But it did. I wanted to be the best drug addict I could be. I wanted, at all costs, to avoid knowing myself and being vulnerable. I had wasted my youth. I'd blossomed into a toxic young man. A sick young man. I survived psychosis. I survived drugs. I survived suicide attempts. I survived jails and rehabs. At what point will my luck run out? How much longer can I fake everything?

I had been lying since I was 6 years old. My whole life had been lived inside of a lie, and fake. I had been projecting an image of who I thought I should have been as a person. Self-pity watered my eyes, not for me now, but for that child who held all those secrets in, that 12-year-old boy who felt true sadness and depression for the first time and didn't tell anyone about it. I was angered at the teenager who thought it was cool to do drugs, the kid who danced with the devil just to show everyone he could. And when he turned around, he had found he was actually in hell and all of his friends had followed him. I was angry at the 18-year-old kid Nate, who chose not to cry or ask for help when his best friends were dying all around him, the kid who couldn't stop the drugs and creating pain, even though he knew it was costing him his life. I hated the kid who threw soda in his mother's face in a fit of rage while coming down off of meth. The kid who stood up for methamphetamine, but wouldn't see how badly he was hurting the ones who loved him.

I lay in a jail cell. Empty. No matter how much others love me, it makes no difference. I needed to love myself. I would rebuild myself once again, teach myself to walk and talk like Nathaniel Wilson. I would state how I feel, look deep into myself, and try to make the right decisions. I didn't know right from wrong anymore, but I would try to rely on instinct, on my memories of what I thought was right before it all went wrong. So distant, those memories. Memories of days when all of my problems weren't catastrophic. Days when my problems were worrying about what was cool to wear to school the next day.

I would now stand up for myself when I felt violated. I would look people straight in the eye and not second-guess myself. These were such great ideas, but I didn't know if they were attainable. I would try, though. For fuck's sake, I will finally try, so I don't have to die.

Chapter 6
Recovery . . . And some alcohol

"Sometimes you can only find Heaven by slowly backing away from hell."

— **Carrie Fisher**

I took the well-done, overcooked hamburger off the grill and placed it on the plate. I had been silent the whole day, full of rage. I got out my phone to see if she had texted back. Nothing. She always ignored me when she messed up. I ran from the grill to the kitchen and took the red potatoes out of the oven. I looked into the soup kettle and saw that the soup was overdone and needed to be poured into a container. Everything was piling up around me.

The chaos reminded me of my drug addiction, only somehow there was more structure and incentive. Another order came in through the printer. I ordered the new employee to make the side salad for the order that had just come in and then tagged it with a sarcastic remark about how he was making me get behind. He chuckled, and so did the dishwasher. We relieved tension by talking shit in this kitchen. If work wasn't fun, then I'd make it fun, or I'd pick on someone newer then me until I felt like it was fun

The waitress breezed by the kitchen window and headed toward the grill. Her head was tilted back and she walked with pride.

She'd better not hassle me over shit right now. I'm not normally this snotty.

I was having a bad night, trying to break up with my girlfriend, but she wouldn't respond. I'm a better alcoholic than a drug addict. I had been clean, off drugs, for a year and a half. I had a good hold on life. I might have been crazy, but not stupid. I had been through enough on the streets to know how to handle liquor and what's acceptable. I drank and drove last night, but only to get away from my girlfriend. I packed up all my things that morning so I could move out. She would be shocked when she discovered that I was serious. I had been through hell with drugs and wasn't going to play her game.

I got the soup out of the kettle and then cleaned the inside. The steel wool heated up and burned my hand, but I liked it. I liked the burn and the pain. I couldn't cut my wrists or slit my throat anymore when I was stressed, so I'd settle for a burn on the tips of my fingers. Another order came through. This restaurant was a blessing for my psychosis. I was so stressed out all the time that I didn't have time to be insane.

"Just back off and let me get this, rookie," I said sarcastically to the new boot.

This restaurant was a blessing for my confidence. I moved up quickly and worked harder than I had ever worked before. I had finished my community service a couple years prior while working two jobs. I started off working at Domino's, when I was fresh out of jail, to please my probation officer. Then I got a second job to make more money. But before doing all of that, I did community service in the mornings. Some days were 15 to 16 hours long. Eventually, it lightened up to something more manageable. I had just been taken off of Antabuse by my probation officer and was drinking more frequently again.

As I folded the order ticket and put it on the ticket line, I saw the watery eyes of my girlfriend, Carol, through the kitchen window.

"Hold on a sec, I'll be out in a minute," I told her.

I prepared all the nasty things I had to say and walked out to lay right into her. My words rolled off of my tongue perfectly. It was too easy. She had messed up in every way possible. It felt good knowing that it wasn't me anymore. She was still teary-eyed and didn't say a word. I reviewed all of the events from last night and reiterated why I was justified in leaving her. She didn't argue. I got to the point and, almost out of breath, I paused.

"I'm pregnant," Carol said.

Everything stopped. Every problem disappeared. Words escaped me. My numb sense of reality had just been shocked back to life. I'd never felt this before. I thought I had felt almost everything, but not this. Fear. Distinct fear. I was 22 years old, and I was not prepared to be a daddy. I wasn't even off of probation yet. I was still just a hurt, 16-year-old boy in my head.

"Okay, are you sure?" I asked.

"I took three different tests and they all said positive," she said.

"Okay . . ." I said blankly.

She asked what we were going to do. I told her I didn't know.

I went back to work to finish my shift. I didn't speak a word. I didn't look up. I did my work but stayed inside of my head. If I broke up with her, would she abort our baby? I had been a stepfather to her then 1 ½-year-old for a year now.

My haze from the hangover started to disappear and I started thinking of possibility and opportunity, facing the problem head on. A new Nate was here nowadays, a Nate who didn't cower from problems. What if I had my own child? I wasn't high on drugs anymore, and I knew how to love now, because I was better at loving myself. I didn't run anymore; that was not me. I was scared, but not a coward. The voices in my head stirred at times, but I learned how to control them. They were not me, but they were mine. I used them to reason, having rational conversations with them instead of listening to random screams and disturbing sentences that used to make me cringe. They were my guilty conscience, and I knew through them when I living in fear.

I knew what love and faith felt like, so I used that to figure out my current dilemma. To be a father or not to be a father? Images of myself holding a baby who's a part of me flowed through my head. My pain subsided, and my anger toward Carol disappeared. Just me and my baby. It's a possibility, isn't it? Seven and a half months from now, I could have the biggest life-changing experience since that day I went crazy at the hospital, except this one would be the opposite. This would be positive. This would be my remedy. This would be a reason to live. My mind was setting itself upon a goal now, accepting a new reality. My fear and anxiety turned into a positive, anxious feeling.

I became excited. I felt I deserved this, and this growing baby deserved my love. I knew what it was like to hate, and I can teach this child how to love. I can teach him or her all I know about what to do and what not to do. I can protect my baby. The decision was made now, in my mind. I have to protect my child by talking with Carol. I called her and told her everything was going to be okay.

I convinced myself of this; I could still convince myself of anything. It was how I'd gotten clean. I convinced myself I was okay when I wasn't. I lied for a while until it became true. I told myself the voices in my head weren't me. I told myself I was worth something when my better judgement told me I was still a piece-of shit-junkie. I lied until it happened. I became what I had programmed myself to be through relentless self-talk.

She believed me when I said it would be okay. I had a feeling deep in my gut that things would go bad again, but I knew if I was going to be a father I had to persevere. We invited my mother over and told her the news. She was shocked. I saw fear in her. I didn't care either. I was going to have a baby. I was going to be a father. I have no idea why I wasn't scared anymore. This was the biggest commitment I had ever made. This was the biggest life event I had ever confronted. I was 22 years old and felt like I hadn't succeeded in anything since I was 16 years old.

I was a good stepfather, but still a drunk. It had come to my attention that I was addicted to porn as well, a nice little gift my twisted meth addiction had left behind with me. That tore my girlfriend and me apart just as badly as the booze would. I was stronger, but still emotionally immature. I was only just partially recovering. Alcohol wasn't as warping to my mind as meth and heroin had been, but it still kept me from my truths. However, when life events call for you to rise up and be strong, you don't have a choice. There's no time to wrap your head around what's about to happen, you just do it. It doesn't matter what the situation is. Success and thriving is a choice, not something you fall into.

My Son, Solomon Lee Wilson

My first memory of things being calm was around the holidays. The third trimester was here, and there was no choice but to accept our situation. I went to work every day, and my smile got bigger. I was getting excited for my baby to come. My son. I had so many abandonment issues from all my friends who were either dead or in jail, or from people who'd left me to use meth.

My son will always love me. He will always be my son. He will never not be my son, as long as I am a good father and put him first. What an awesome concept. I have someone to live for now. Someone I would die for, too. Someone I would do anything for—and I haven't even seen his face. My own problems faded. My relationship was going great. She was finally happy and accepted that we were going to have a baby. We communicated. I quit looking at porn, and I quit drinking, except for special occasions. I almost felt normal.

My son's due date was January 10. The holidays passed, and the good times were slowing down. One day, I was playing in the living room with AJ, my stepson, when Carol burst through the door in panic and exclaimed "I either peed my pants or my water broke!"

This was it! We rushed to the hospital and spent the whole day waiting. The contractions increased then decreased, then increased and decreased. A part of me wanted to go home, and I'm sure she did, too.

Friends came and left, and close family stayed. The sun was setting, and the contractions increased again. The baby was coming.

It happened so fast. The nurses rushed in with the doctor. I stood and watched. Everyone moved so fast around me, in a blur. I sat there, stuck in the moment. It was almost like a near-overdose, except it felt good instead of scary. Then he just popped out, just like that. The doctor nearly dropped him. He was purple, and the umbilical cord was wrapped around his neck. I cut the cord and held him and listened to him cry. Yes, I cried, too.

It was so cliché for me to sit there and cry, and say everything had changed in that moment, but it was true. I saw the piece of me that died on the streets come back to life that day. God gave back what I had lost and rewarded me for being strong and surviving. I sat there in silence, holding my son and a piece of my heart. Reluctantly, I gave him back to the nurses to be cleaned and wrapped up. I spent the night sleeping at the hospital, not wanting to leave my son's side.

I changed his diapers and helped as much as I could. I loved every minute of it. I wanted a hand in whatever was being done to take care of my son. He was my why for everything now: I took care of myself so I could take care of him. I worked so I could support him. I stayed clean and took care of my emotions so I could be stable and take care of him.

The weeks that followed were just as joyful as the last trimester in Carol's pregnancy. We remained stable and worked hard and loved hard. We had a family.

As time went on, alcohol slowly made its way into our lives again. It started off the same as my drug addiction had. It seemed like a good idea or like everything is under control enough to manage it.

"It'd be nice to have a night out, huh?" I said to Carol, like I hadn't had enough nights out in my life yet. Like nothing in my life could possibly give me the relief that alcohol does. Unfortunately, there *is* no replacement for what a substance can give you. But that's just the point, too.

We started drinking a few times a week. My birthday came, and she threw me a surprise kegger. It was a blast. All my friends were there, all the friends I had gone through so much with. Everything was still perfect. I was clean and free of drugs and had planned to live out my days being an alcoholic and a family man. I kind of saw this as being the

American way, or at least the Woodland Park way. I figured we had all been through so much, there was no way we were going to continue our lives without at least being alcoholics.

Sure, I'll start following your stupid laws and following all of that bullshit protocol I never wanted to follow before, but I will be drunk in the evenings

I was still a good father: Good, but not the best. You can't be the best when you're hungover, but you can still be good if you try. Hell, most of America lives like this, I reasoned. The kids are still young enough I can present myself as a hero and a respectable figure without them realizing my flaws and without them seeing my underlying hurt from the past. I was happy, though. I was where I was supposed to be.

The Family Breaks

My surprise birthday party was the last memory of a good night with Carol. We moved on, went to work every day, and our drinking increased. I told her we should stop. I saw the arguments growing and the toxicity in our relationship increasing. She wanted to, and I wanted to, but it didn't happen. I told her we needed to go at least three days without drinking. We would go one night without drinking, and then she'd come home with Jägermeister, and we would drink. Inevitably, an argument would ensue. She would leave and go to Manitou Springs to hang out at the 24-hour tea shop. At first, we would both apologize for the night before, until the frequency became too high and we gave up.

The day came when I finished my probation. No more probation officer. No more breathalyzers or UAs. Freedom! This was the first time since I was 14 that I didn't have an ongoing case or probation or been in the system. I felt accomplished. I imagine most people would view that condition as just being normal, but I saw triumph and a new future. I had had so many cases, hours of community service, and court dates hanging over my head for the past 8 years; it was like letting go of a heavy weight.

To celebrate the end of my probation, we bought beer and drank it. Even though life was better than on drugs, our arguments were at an all-time high. We couldn't spend an hour together without arguing. No matter what she said, I would fire back and retaliate. I didn't care anymore. No more stopping the drinking, no more repairing and apologizing and changing. I gave up. From being a drug addict, I knew how to change to apathy very quickly. I can turn sick anytime. I can still hide in my psychosis if I choose to. I can talk to the voices in my head about how much I hate you. I can look at the scars on my forearm and my neck and hide in the pain of my past instead of moving forward. And that's what I shall do.

I can drink and still handle my child, I thought to myself. I can drink all night and still wake up when he cries and give him formula. I can be the "perfect alcoholic." I lulled myself into this delusion. I had accepted years ago that alcohol seemed like such a miniscule substance compared to injecting speed balls. I knew that if I chose to I could remain drunk for the rest of my life. I accepted that I would most likely choose alcohol to medicate, because I could not get high on meth and heroin anymore. I knew I would likely choose alcohol over getting therapy, because it was easier, more immediate, and legal. I knew I would choose alcohol over love because it understood me more than a significant other ever could. I'll choose alcohol over sex, because I can stay drunk for longer than I can have sex, and it's just easier. Alcohol filled up those cracks in my heart. It brought relief to anxiety. Alcohol made it easier to deal with my relationship with Carol.

We had argued all week, mostly because porn had come back into the picture. Both of us had silently but mutually accepted that we would choose alcohol over repairing our relationship. She would come home after work when I was with my son Solomon. Then I would wait to drink until after she would start a fight and leave, so I could blame her.

Carol came home one day and said "I'm going out tonight, and I'm not coming back tonight."

"Cool," I said apathetically. I would get excited every time she left because I knew I'd be alone with my son. Peaceful and drunk. That night, I spent the night watching movies and drinking. Then I got a call at about 2 in the morning. It was Carol.

"I'm coming home. I'm sorry about everything, I want to make things better," she said with sensitivity.

I knew better though, as I spoke through the filter of the alcohol. I told her not to come home. I told her to stay with a friend. If she truly wants to make things better, she can wait until the morning when we are sober. I told her not to drink and drive, but she insisted on coming home. I went straight to bed hoping to dodge the battle I knew would inevitably be coming.

I awoke to a voice above me. I decided to get up and give it a chance. We talked and talked. From years of drug use, I can see moments when rationality is present and when a substance has control over my mind, even when I am under the influence. It's as though I can look down on myself when I'm intoxicated and see, almost from a third-person point of view, that rationality is leaving and the alcohol is starting to win.

The talking turned into arguing and finger pointing. Tolerance was low on both sides, and the noise and friction and tension increased. Her voice got too loud and I knew I needed to leave. I told her I was leaving and she began striking me with her fists. I caught a punch above my eye. I was still not angry, but was defensive. As I turned and headed for the door, and I felt fists hit the back of my head. *Now I'm fucking angry.* She tried to punch more, and I grabbed her wrists and threw her onto the couch. She lay there and cried out for a second. I guessed she was pretending I'd hit her. If she pretended something hard enough, she could usually convince herself that it happened. I knew I needed to get out of the house. I saw my chance to leave and bolted for the door. I heard her behind me, screaming. Not yelling, but screaming. She called me a pervert and a porn addict and a drug addict.

She was throwing things as I made it to my car. I could see her get inside hers too. She started her car quicker and blocked me into the driveway. Her car was now sideways, as she was facing the driveway. My rage set in as I shifted my car into reverse. I slowly backed up and nudged my bumper softly against her driver's-side door. She slammed her fists on the window and screamed at the top of her lungs. I pulled the car forward and parked it.

"GET OUT AND TALK TO ME LIKE A MAN!" She paused for a second and disappeared.

She popped out of the blackness and I saw her hands raised above her head, holding a small boulder the size of a basketball.. She slammed the rock hard against my window. I flipped it in reverse again and get as close to her car as I can.

"Move your car!" I screamed.

The rock hit my window again. *The window wouldn't hold for much longer.* I pulled my car forward and turned off the ignition. Maybe I can reason with . . .

Then the rock shattered my back window.

I sat helpless in my car. Then I did the one thing I hate doing—I called the cops. She was screaming in the background. Her voice made my neck stand up, and my head felt like it was shrinking inward. I wasn't even mad anymore; I was beaten up and sad. She had no idea what she had done. Alcohol was like kryptonite for her. Maybe it was the Native American in her, or maybe it was childhood issues resurfacing. When the cops came, Carol was still screaming and yelling.

"He's a drug addict! He used to do heroin!!" she bellowed.

I let her do all the talking. Finally, she calmed down. As the police talked to both of us, I got the feeling I was going to jail the more and more they talked. Neither of the cops wanted to take me in, but in a domestic situation they have to take somebody. She was calming down. She asked them to hurry up, so we could figure out who has to watch the kid tomorrow while I'm in jail. I saw them talking amongst themselves and then they approached me.

Jail...Again

"We're taking you in for criminal tampering domestic violence," they explained.

Repeat offender. Here we go again. Handcuffs and Miranda rights. Same shit. Reminds me of another time when I was arrested while I was doing community service. No remorse, just a feeling of helplessness that I had become accustomed to: Doing my best, but being so deep in a hole it didn't matter. My most valiant efforts could not deter the curse I had placed on myself from doing drugs and drinking—or, in this case, staying in a relationship longer than I should have. My cell phone stayed in my pocket, and I managed to get it out despite being handcuffed. I texted my mother and told her I'd be in jail in a few hours. The officer hopped into the car and we started driving. He stopped a block away from where I lived, in front of the restaurant where I worked.

"I need a smoke break," he said. "Can you smoke in handcuffs?"

"I'll make it work," I said.

He gave me a cigarette. I held it in the corner of my mouth and puffed it when I needed a drag.

"So, I'm taking you in and you're getting arraigned tomorrow. I have no idea what your bail will be, but it will be set tomorrow," he explained.

I saw remorse in his face for arresting me. He explained he normally worked down on B Street, a street that was a marker for lower-income neighborhood. He told me he had seen some hard shit. I think he was trying to give me an inspirational speech on staying out of trouble. He obviously didn't know who I was. I chuckled on the inside and thought it was cute.

"I don't necessarily think you belong in jail, but someone has to go to jail," he explained.

I told him I knew and that I was relieved, because it gave me a way out of this relationship. We finished the smoke and headed to CJC. I went through the booking process, saw some old, ugly mug shots from when I was on meth, and then finally made it to bed in the middle of the night, after hours in booking.

I could hear that breakfast had arrived, but fuck that. I was hungover and needed more rest. I slept until about 11 and my court hearing was at 1. I walked like a zombie through the halls and arrived at video court. I didn't pay attention to anyone else. I didn't care about the other cases. They were reminders of a life I was leaving behind.

I heard the other inmates gossip all morning about their cases and how bad they were and what their excuses for doing it were, or how they got fucked over and they're innocent. I didn't care anymore. And of course, just like every other time, I saw some youngster who thinks it's cool to be in jail and makes stupid jokes, and looked like he was actually enjoying himself in this pit.

I went through the video arraignment and had my bail set, as usual. I called my father, and he said they will bail me out. I waited and waited a few hours, doing my best to avoid talking to anyone. As I was being released, the punk kid who thinks it's cool to be in jail stepped in front of me, thinking I'm ready to joke around.

"Where you think you're going, bro?" he asked sarcastically.

"Get the fuck out of my way," I replied.

I breezed past him like he was an ant and got my mattress and all my other toiletries. I was now broken up with Carol; she just didn't know it yet. I suddenly had a more empowered, take-no-shit attitude. That part felt good, but I was full of rage. I had a chip on my shoulder again. My son was not in my custody and I'd been ripped from my home. I had become a new person now. She didn't know it yet. No one did.

Something clicked inside of me in jail. I wasn't going to be nice anymore. I wasn't going to be walked on. I'm not taking shit from anybody. I'm being me. I made my way through booking again, and my mother picked me up. We talked and talked some more. Like old times, we made it home, and I went to sleep.

An Alcoholic's Escape

After this incident, it made it easy for me to justify being an alcoholic. I was never "out of control" when drinking. I could always point the finger at my ex and say, "I'm not like her." I continued to drink for years to come. I went from being a cook to working in a sheet metal shop, then being laid off, and then working for a friend setting tile. I worked for the YMCA and got paid as little as an employer could possibly pay you. I eventually quit that job, too.

I drank through all those years. I was a good father, but chose drinking over my son some nights. I did grow during that time, though. I became more confident and learned more every day. One night during those years of drinking, I relapsed once on heroin; but other than that I stayed clean, off of the hard drugs, except for alcohol.

During the years I worked as a cook, I had a blast. I got the chance to relive those moments I'd missed out on when I was on drugs. I grew in confidence and excelled in cooking. I was given a large bonus by my boss after working 60+ hours a week for a month straight. This was the first time I can remember feeling like I kicked ass at life. This was the hardest I had ever worked. I partied just the same.

I'd finally figured out a way to deal with my past: Wear it with pride. I quit being ashamed that I was an addict and actually took some pride in my recovery. Others disagreed and, yes, I was still very emotionally flawed, but the growth started there. I was still young and obnoxious, but that was okay. It didn't make me a scumbag. All that happiness I used to practice years ago when my recovery had first started was beginning to become real.

Unwanted anger and sadness issues arose as well. Nights without my son were hard, and I didn't let myself heal properly from that breakup. The drinking didn't allow me to drop the chip on my shoulder.

Recovery, for me, was not a straight line. I relapsed, not only on substances and continuing to drink, but also on having a bad attitude. I hung around other convicts and addicts who had seen the same sides of life that I had. I felt that people like us had a special understanding of the hardships of life and had an edge the average person didn't know about.

Drawing out the Positive

There are bad sides to addiction, but it also has the side that others don't know about. There are the good things you learn, like how to survive, be adaptable, and how to overcome trauma. After I became a certified personal trainer, I was told once in a job interview for a big-box gym that I "thrived in chaos." I liked hearing that. I knew where I picked up that trait. I learned it from having to survive. In drug addiction, I chose drugs over everything and had a passion for getting drugs despite everything seeming to crumble around me.

When I got clean, I had to use this survival tool to thrive in a chaotic work environment. This started with working as a cook in a restaurant. This was not an average kitchen. This kitchen had a reputation for chewing up and spitting out chefs, cooks, and servers who didn't have the heart to keep up. My buddy Lee, years ago, had sat tentatively and listened to me, over and over again, shuffling through my schizophrenic concepts and phrases I would spit out in my schizophrenic mindset.

One day he replied simply, "Yeah, but once you get through this, you'll be tough as nails, bro!"

I stopped and pondered the simple but sturdy statement he had made. I didn't believe him then. I wasn't even sure whether he believed I would live past the next year, but he was right. I started seeing this statement become true in the years of my early recovery and began to master it as I became seasoned. I thrived in the kitchen, and probably could have done better if I hadn't been drinking, but the timing for me to quit was not there yet.

My psychosis was very controlled now. The delusions started to morph into something I could identify as anxiety and, therefore, manage better. I still had voices in my head, but if stayed busy enough and carried myself with a stature of confidence, they seemed to disappear. Every once in a while, on a hangover, they might get louder and my thoughts more rapid, but I still managed to keep my eyes forward and my head up.

I learned about controlling anxiety and taking charge of my mind. It was all about perspective. I learned that anxiety and excitement light up the same area in your brain. They both release cortisol, and they both increase your pulse. I learned about this from being in so many therapy classes and even learned a little bit more about cortisol from school. Again, it's just a matter of perspective. Once I learned that my random anxiety attacks were just pent up energy, my life changed. To deter anxiety, I had to take action and use that energy to make the pain stop.

When I would feel a rush of anxiety or my thoughts would become too rapid to handle, I would take a step back and analyze the situation and see what actions I could take to use this excess energy that seemed to be overwhelming me. Sometimes, I would have to sift through my train of thought and pinpoint what thought or emotion might have triggered this. If I was in the middle of work, and I thought of something that had happened in my past that made me angry and I started to feel overwhelmed, I could identify myself with that emotion and start to cope with it. This took a lot of mental strength, but was completely necessary to overcome my psychosis and anxiety.

I had to come to internal peace with the fact that the thoughts I was having weren't some split personality or some other being in control of my mind; it was me! That concept was devastating at first. Looking back to when Xaq had just died, and I was using so many drugs and I couldn't tell which way was up, I believe something in me changed. I had more disturbing thoughts and had bad intentions that I was not familiar with. The trauma of losing my friend had disturbed me. I didn't want to face it. I convinced myself that I had another person in my head, so I didn't have to face this new and damaged person I had become. I wasn't taking charge of my mind and my emotions. I let the voices take charge and emotions run rampant, and that turned into psychosis and a schizophrenic mindset.

Anxiety was my brain's way of forcing me to take charge and take action. If my efforts to talk, deal with problems, advance in life, or be a better person were minimal, my anxiety was maximal and was going to take charge of my life for me.

Plateau

I decided after three years in the restaurant that I had hit a plateau spiritually and financially. I just wasn't challenged anymore. If I didn't make a change, I would likely end up cooking and getting drunk the rest of my life. I knew my winter hours would always get cut, and I wasn't willing to kiss enough asses to pass the one person who was higher in command than me. It was as a coworker and I would say, "We need big-boy jobs!" As soon as I knew I didn't want to work at the restaurant anymore, I searched through job possibilities day in and day out. My work ethic did fall a bit or maybe just shifted from the task at hand. I spent more energy on finding another job and became less available and dedicated to my current job. I became unfocused and selfish, and somewhat entitled. Looking back, this may be something I would have worked on a bit more. But still, I searched onward.

In looking for a new job, I sold myself short and told myself I wasn't capable of doing some things because of my record and my past. I had two felonies and two DUIs. While this may have been a setback, I had no idea what my potential was, because I had set boundaries on what was possible. Because I had seen so many people in recovery settle for jobs they didn't want, I thought that was just normal. I thought working in a sheet metal shop and learning how to weld might be a good option for me. Even if my police record didn't get in the way, I had told myself for years now:

Regular people don't understand you. You've been through too much. You have too much trauma on your brain. You will have to be around other addicts and convicts the rest of your life.

Sometimes, these statements were true. Sometimes I preferred to be around a fellow addict than another "normal" person. There's a mindset and certain level of respect among people who have been to prison or people who have been on the streets that others sometimes don't get. But for years, over and over, I underestimated my potential by using this thought process.

I began work in the sheet metal shop in September 2012. I had no clue what I was doing. I learned how to sheer metal and drive a forklift. I got good at the forklift through trial and error. There was an incident where I accidentally swiped the back door to the building with the forklift. The forklift was a bright neon green and the color of my mistake gleamed proudly on the backdoor for everyone to see.

I liked the people I worked with, for the most part. I told a youngster off a couple of times, but that was typical anywhere I went. I found myself becoming a little more hostile as I stayed clean longer. I had been clean of illicit drugs for about 4 years now. I still drank, though, and it fueled my misguided anger sometimes. After a few months of working in the shop, my happiness did not increase as much as I thought it would. I didn't get trained well, likely because I wasn't a quick learner when it came to measuring and cutting sheet metal and learning the machines. Every day I went to work, I felt a little more behind, like I wasn't picking things up quickly enough or like the boss wasn't satisfied with my work. I didn't know what to do differently or what questions to ask.

I took a look at what I was good at or what I had passion for. A year earlier I had started going to the gym regularly. I went every day. Hung over, sober, didn't matter. It just clicked with me. It was my new therapy and my new nourishment for staying off of drugs, and it forced me to cut way back on drinking. When thinking of new career routes, after digging deep and deciding I had no place in a sheet metal shop, I decided that being a personal trainer would be best for me. I had no idea how much money they made or where I was going to work once I became certified, but I started taking courses at a small technical school in Colorado Springs. Somehow, my employer caught wind of this. Some days at work I would picture myself getting laid off and kind of look forward to it in my head, though I didn't want to admit it.

My boss asked casually one day, "So, you're taking courses for physical training, huh?"

"Yeah, I am!" I tried not to sound surprised.

I didn't want to tell anyone I worked with because I didn't trust that I wouldn't get fired for it.

"That's awesome, man. I wish I could do that," he sounded enthused for me.

A few weeks went by and my work ethic, like before, began to decline once I had found another passion. I found myself calling in sick some days and going to the gym instead of working. Eventually, I fulfilled my subconscious fantasy of getting laid off. I felt down a little bit, but somewhat excited. Mad at the employer, but relieved. Life has a funny way of playing itself out.

Within a few weeks, I was collecting unemployment and working for my buddy setting tile and doing restorative construction. He paid well, and I loved working with a friend. But like before, I felt like I just plain sucked at anything that was construction-related. I still attended classes at the technical school and still made it to the gym every day. My drinking stayed about the same.

A few months after that, the tile business was slowing down and I hardly had any hours. I spent lots of time being angry at myself for not being able to succeed in the work field. My moods fluctuated frequently, so even though I was excited about becoming a trainer, I was still in panic about how to make immediate money. I chose to think of myself as a helpless, recovering addict and felon. My love life seemed to fall in the crapper as well. Every woman I asked out on a date either gave me the wrong number, wouldn't respond to my texts or calls, or wanted to play games.

I was at a different low. I got belligerently drunk in a downtown bar the night before Thanksgiving and got into a fight. I was too drunk and didn't keep my guard up, and ended up with a black eye and a busted lip. The other guy didn't get a scratch on him. I showed up to Thanksgiving dinner really hungover and beat up. It wasn't my first fight and wouldn't be the last. My unemployment ran out and so did all of the tile work.

I applied for a job in the gym at the YMCA in downtown Colorado Springs. I had a friend who worked there and she helped me get my foot in the door. Getting a job there was not easy. I had to go through a few orientations and a few meetings that sometimes lasted a couple hours. I got CPR training, too. Then, because of my record, I had to go to their corporate office and explain why I had a record and why I was doing better since then. I did all this for just a little above minimum wage and about 28 hours a week! It was a necessary means to an end, I decided.

Around this time in my life, I started drinking even more because I had lots of idle time and had been associating with more convicts and more gang members. I hung around with some of the toughest in Colorado Springs. I was the nice guy of the crowd, but my attitude started changing. I was going through the cycle I always went through, this time using alcohol instead of drugs. I was frustrated with being broke and had to move back in with my parents since getting laid off a few months prior. I started hanging around the biker bars and the dive bars.

I thought of these as some of the best times of my life. I drank for free and got a lot of female attention because of the people I associated with and my bad-boy attitude. There were some negatives AND positives to this time in my life and they were important to my growth. Until this time, I had always figured that meth and other drugs had taken my confidence away from me for good. I was still ashamed of the things I had done and seen. I watched the way these convicts and gangsters carried themselves. They did what they wanted and acted how they wanted. *If you don't like it, then fuck you* was their motto. They were seasoned and had been through more institutions and violence than I had. I picked up on this and decided that not giving a fuck was easier. This was not only a partial relapse of old behavior but also a necessary characteristic to actually overcoming my past problems with esteem and confidence.

I was the way I was. That's it. That simple. I don't deserve to be disrespected. I deserved things I wasn't getting, even in my recovery. That was the reason I had let myself be abused in past relationships. That was the reason I wasn't as aggressive as I needed to be in the work field. That's the reason I settled for jobs I didn't want. That was the reason I wasn't attracting the woman of my dreams. That was the reason I didn't have fun in social settings. This new attitude changed everything. I had the most fun I'd ever had the summer of 2014.

After a few months, I quit the YMCA. I just texted and told her I wasn't showing up. I told her I knew that was immature, but I didn't feel that the job was mature enough anyway. Looking back, I should have put in two weeks' notice, but quitting the job was a good move.

One of the downsides was that I was over confident. I didn't care about consequences, and I was hostile to the outside world. I was living in an anti-social bubble again, like when I had done drugs. I'd say my only pro-social outlets were going to work, which was only for a small paycheck, and whatever social activity I had at the bars and clubs, which was questionable in itself. I found myself in more confrontations and more fights than ever before, and I was comfortable with that. I felt like I had discovered in myself a warrior that had been dormant for years. In early sobriety, I had been passive, but gradually escalated into a hostile, confrontational but more confident man.

Bad Company

I eventually got a new job working in a bar. This bar had a reputation for being a tough bar. Bikers went frequently. This bar also had rap nights where shootings, stabbings, and fights were not out of the norm. It was a blast at first. I would get to meet all of the respected gangsters who would come in. Seeing some of the bikers I had seen on *Gangland* in real life and shaking their hands made me feel big and proud. It was the same as a kid meeting his favorite sports star, only for an aspiring criminal. The summer was coming to its end, and all of our fun was coming to an end, too. It seemed like everyone from my crew was getting ready to go to prison.

My buddy, Randy, who was trying to stay clean, had relapsed and was speed balling and getting into the drug game again. He said he didn't care because he was going to prison, even though his sentence had been reduced to 10 years from 25. I had three or four other friends who were already in prison or soon to go back. I was being left behind again. Just like my friends who had died years back, only this time they were all going to prison. Night after night, I saw less and less of my friends and found myself alone, working in the bar on the weekends and going out by myself, trying to relive those wild and crazy nights we had had together.

On a cool night in October, I had been let go from work early due to slow business. I made my way down to my other regular bar just outside of the downtown strip. Randy was running the bar and getting me discounted drinks the whole night. I was having a blast and so were a few others, but it just wasn't the same that night. Randy was tending the bar, high on heroin, and didn't have much energy to put into socializing with us.

Later another friend showed up, strung out on meth. No one was smiling much, and the laughs did not come as often as they should have. A younger kid came in and was getting belligerent and disrespecting every other male in the bar. Eventually he got kicked out, and we told him to go far away from here because this was the wrong crowd to be messing with. In his drunken stupor, he circled back while Randy and I were outside smoking cigarettes. We told him to get lost one more time, and I took off my hat to get ready to fight him. Before I could get to him, my buddy Marky flew by me, grabbed him by the throat, and put him down with one punch. The kid was light work for a guy like Marky.

The rest of the night was filled with more people yelling and fights being broken up. Finally, Randy had cleaned up the bar and we started to head home. I was headed southbound on Interstate 25 in Colorado Springs, talking with Randy about life, addiction, and how he was preparing for prison. He had no more care in his voice. At the beginning of spring, when he had first gotten clean, he was full of jokes and spark and charisma. Heroin and the legal system had sucked it dry.

My exit was coming up quickly and I cut across two lanes within 50 yards to make it over. In my rearview mirror, I saw something that I hadn't seen in about 6 years . . . cop lights.

"Are you getting pulled over?" Randy asked with despair in his voice that I had felt in my heart.

The Last Chance

All these years of getting out of the system and time spent not drinking and driving, and building my life with my son, and building my life from nothing was hanging by a thread in this moment. I felt more angry than scared. I knew this was coming. I was living like a thug, and I was lucky that things didn't end up worse. I ended up in cuffs again in the back of the cop car.

I didn't go to jail this time because I opted to take a blood test at the hospital. I was back almost where I had started. For some reason, I was more comfortable this time. Partially because I had been in trouble so many times before, or maybe it was because I knew this was bound to happen given the people I was associating with. But a weird instinct told me that I was going to be okay through it all.

I went to a lawyer and he looked over my case. "Well, your record is not good at all, but it's not the worst I've seen," he said calmly. "There may be a jurisdiction issue, but we can't guarantee that," he explained.

Hope. But a part of me knew better than to hope. Hope had always got me kicked in the face. You always look at the worst-case scenario and count on that. Then there's no let down. "If you're convicted, you're looking at 60 days minimum," he said.

Not as bad as I had thought. Not bad at all for having two prior felonies and two prior DUIs. I wasn't looking forward to jail, but I was still mostly calm about my situation. One thing, one painful thought lingered in the back of my head, though. Leaving my son was something I wasn't sure I could forgive myself for. Inside that thought lived a million other insecurities that I kept tame, thoughts of getting lost inside of jail, associating with people who were fresh off the streets from doing meth and heroin and robbing, and all those things my evil side loved to take part in. That's the part I feared about this situation.

But I maintained. I chose not to fly off of the handle. I ended getting a new job doing heating and air conditioning, because working only on weekends in the bar wasn't working. It was a nice snap back to reality. I didn't have as much fun as I did in the bar, but it was more practical, and it paid for my lawyer. The guys I worked with were mostly assholes, which fit me well considering how I had been acting for the past few years. I cut my drinking to the weekends only, when I was working in the bar. Eventually, when I became more financially stable, I quit my job in the bar. Looking back, that job did next to nothing for me. It barely paid me, and it did not challenge me to grow at all.

The downside to my new job was that I had to drop out of school and dedicate myself strictly to HVAC until I could get more stable. The days were long, and as time went on I hated the people I worked with more and more. My court date for sentencing was repeatedly delayed, but I was okay with that. I was in no rush to get back into county jail. I let my bitterness dwell inside of me because I knew I was going back in. I knew I needed that hate to fit in inside of jail.

The days got harder and longer. My tolerance for my coworkers was growing thin, and I was contemplating seriously hurting someone. I saw the way one of my coworkers had tolerated it for a few years now: He went to work during the day and got drunk every night. A part of me wanted that. I had lived that for years. He settled. I knew it would be an easy move to settle like that. It reminded me of how I used to be. But day after day, I was being pulled in a different direction. Also, I was being pushed out by the negativity of the company, to choose something better. I was being confronted with a decision.

After about 8 months of working for the HVAC company, I injured my back when I lifted a wheelbarrow full of stones. I could barely sit up and walked hunched over for about a week. After 2 weeks, it started to get a little better, but I was angry. My workouts had now been hindered by this job, and that was the last straw. This job was taking my soul, and now it was about to put the one thing that gave me relief outside of work in jeopardy. That's more than I could accept.

After 9 months on the job, I gave my 2-week notice and went back to school—the best decision I ever made. This was what separated me from settling for an average life and the life I have now. The decision took me a while to make and it was scary, but I knew that if I was sentenced I wouldn't be given work release, and I would just do straight time. I did take into account that my case might be dismissed based on the cop being out of his jurisdiction when he pulled me over. This was a huge risk for me because I was afraid I wouldn't see my son for months at a time if convicted. The stress of this decision was like none before. I was a changed man. I was a father. I was almost done with school and about to make a career. Going to jail would set me so far back, and the emotional pain of leaving my son might be something I wasn't sure I could recover from.

I finished school a couple weeks before my final court date. I remained calm; I felt content for some weird reason. All of my old friends were in prison, I had just broken up with my girlfriend, and I had absolutely no job. The party was finally over. But I knew something was going to go right for me, because I was listening to my calling.

It was around this time that I started to believe in God again. I did partially in the past, but I had so much anger against Him and there were times I would deny Him because of that. I would deny Him whenever things would go badly in my life. I got off on hating Him. He was my scapegoat. I was finding a balance in what I actually believed in and what had been forced upon me when I was younger.

I noticed everything in my life went wrong when I quit believing. My head would fall out of order or things felt out of control. I found who God was to me. It wasn't the God I was raised to believe in. I decided I would need a much more forgiving God. I needed a God who wouldn't judge me. So I created my faith, and I thrived because of it.

God had a plan for me this year. Recapping what had happened that year, I learned that even though I had blown off school and settled for jobs that didn't challenge me or weren't right for me, that I had grown mentally. I learned, from convicts, how to carry myself with confidence. Something that small and simple changed my whole perspective on my actions. At first, I felt entitled and arrogant. After working in the bar, drinking for free, and getting all the attention I wanted from the opposite sex, I felt like I was owed something from the world. But after shaping up to prepare for the DUI sentence, I was humbled and was taught that I needed to fight for what I have. I had been through so much in my life. I knew that even though I might be headed for jail, I was going to get the job I wanted and work for something I believed in. Fitness!

The final court date came. I exited the elevator, made my way to the bench outside the courtroom, and waited for my lawyer. I saw the DA meeting with the arresting officer. They stood there with tension and panic in their voices. I liked it. It felt like revenge for when I was in a similar situation when I was 15 and the cops went to their cars to fumble through their law book, just like they were now.

"Well, he still committed a crime!" the cop said with desperation.

The judge dismissed my case. I was ecstatic inside. After years and years of bad decisions mixed with bad luck, I was given a break. I was mature enough now in life and my recovery to know that this was an opportunity, not a get-out-of-jail-free card. I was excited but not cocky. I had been humbled.

I didn't go out and celebrate by getting drunk. I scheduled an appointment to take my personal trainer test and studied like hell for 2 weeks. I bought two apps and practiced the questions for at least a couple hours a day until the night before the test. I passed the test with ease. I was a new me. I had absolutely no idea where I would go with this, but I was excited! It reminded me of when I was fresh out of jail in 2009, looking for a new job and a new way to live my life. Only this time, I'm a man.

Chapter 7
Finding Success and Peace

"I knew that I had been partially right in the storeroom above the bar on Christmas Day. Whoever I had become had to die."

Craig Ferguson, *American on Purpose: The Improbable Adventures of an Unlikely Patriot*

With my new fitness certification, I applied at all the big gyms, like 24 Hour Fitness and Gold's Gym. My first interview was at Gold's Gym. They conducted what was called a "practical" interview: one of the employees acts like a client and I take them through a workout. I had no idea what I was doing. They said they liked my personality, but that I didn't have what it took to make sales. The manager, who was a happy-looking guy said, "Look, man, if you're looking to make a lot of money, this isn't the place for you. If you're looking to make a few bucks or help a few people, this is what we do," he said casually.

I believed in the concept of helping people to their goals, but two things didn't make sense: not wanting to make money, and, if I wasn't going to make a lot of money, then I wanted the gratification of helping people on a massive level, neither of which I would find there. So, I then went to 24 Hour Fitness. I completed one personal interview with the manager and another "practical" interview. Again, I wasn't enough of a sales person. My interviewer complimented me on my ability to "thrive under pressure," which motivated me. He liked my ability to switch gears promptly under tension. But in the end it didn't matter what my program design looked like or my dedication toward wanting to help people, it was all about sales—signing up new members...revenue. The manager scheduled another interview, but I didn't show up for it.

Following My Passion

I was beginning to feel like I had made a mistake by quitting my job as an HVAC installer. Every move I made felt like stepping farther into the unknown. It would have been easy for me to go back into the bar and ask for my old job back, and I pondered that at times. But no, I had already tried that lifestyle. I barely ever drank now. I was scared to death of a third DUI. I knew I wouldn't get off easy like I did this last time.

I knew I could have gone back to jobs that I wasn't good at or I didn't enjoy just for a paycheck, but I followed my passion and my heart. In success, I've found that there are many times you will not follow logic or rational thinking. Sometimes you go with your heart.

So, I searched on. I went to the last place on my checklist, ProFit. This was a small gym that was located in a strip mall on the north side of town, in a more affluent neighborhood. I had done my externship there for school, and I liked the gym. I met with the owner, and he immediately hired me. But I noticed there was no one in the gym. When

I had done my externship a few months prior, he had one employee working for him and multiple clients coming in and out of the gym. The gym was hurting for business now.

"It's your job to get people in the door," my new boss said. "I have another job I have to attend to, so you will pretty much be in charge, as long as I can trust you."

Growing

It sounded promising. Maybe not promising for business, but promising for me to grow. This was going to mold me into a smarter trainer, starting from the bottom like this. I was excited for the challenge and a little intimidated, but I didn't care. I had nothing to lose at this point. I decided I had to try hard at something until a new door opened and gave way to my pressure. I had no idea what I was doing, but I started developing the mind of an entrepreneur.

How would I get people in the door? My mind started getting creative for the first time in a long time. Anhedonia had been blocking my creativity for years, and now that I was vulnerable and knew I had nothing to lose I could let my mind run free. My psychosis was no longer psychosis. It was just voices in my head and my thoughts. And they worked *for* me now instead of confusing me. I would sit in the office in complete silence and just think. My best ideas came when I sat there staring at the gym, envisioning what things could look like if I applied myself. I started thinking about fundraisers and different foundations I could partner with to create income for both of us.

I made a call to a Juvenile Diabetes Foundation and began laying the blueprints for a fundraiser called "Pullups for Cash." The inspiration came from my father, who had struggled with diabetes for years. I wanted to start a powerlifting club, too. All these ideas and creativity I never knew I had started flowing out of me. I didn't know I was capable of such vision anymore. I pondered the thought of helping drug addicts and showing them how fitness had helped me, but I didn't want to include my boss in that idea for fear of his judgement of my past. Unfortunately, some of these ideas did not come to fruition, but I believed that the realization of my creative ability was the beginning of something great.

The holidays came and went, and the gym's business was still moving too slowly. The boss was never there and he missed a few appointments I had set up for him for potential clients who wanted nutrition counseling. After New Year's, the busiest time of year in the fitness industry, the phone was shut off. I knew this was the end. I called the boss and told him the phone had been shut off.

"Ok, I'll be working on that," he said with hesitancy. I could tell by the sound of his voice he had no plans of getting the phone turned back on. His voice told me that he was done with the business. He was done with the stress and done with struggling. I couldn't blame him. After that day, I quit coming in for work.

A few weeks earlier, I'd gotten a call from Travis, a fellow trainer in Colorado Springs. He explained that he wanted to network, and I agreed to meet him. He was with an older man, Buckley, and they pitched me their business, which was multi-level marketing (MLM). One of those forbidden pyramid schemes. Years earlier, I nearly got involved with another MLM that involved travel, but I didn't pursue it. This time I saw potential. I saw the charisma in both of their characters as they told me about their business and about their products. I saw opportunity and wanted to try something different that would allow me to be an entrepreneur and still make money through a second endeavor. Plus, I had virtually no personal training clients at the time and had nothing to lose.

Travis also got me into a small studio so that I could build my personal training clientele. Travis and I made great partners, and we brainstormed ways to network for our MLM and who to pitch it to. We blasted people through private Facebook messages, asking them to check out our nutrition company. Sometimes it worked and sometimes it didn't. Some hated us for messaging them and I kind of liked that. It made me feel like an underdog and that I was fighting my way to success. We still drove forward full force and our ravenous hunger for success changed something inside me.

Hungry for Success

This was a new life to me. I had never seen such drive before. In past jobs, it was like I and everyone I worked with were just there for a paycheck and had no passion for what we were doing. This was different. There was a belief behind what we were doing and, of course, a higher sense of urgency since we were young entrepreneurs. It reminded me of how things could have been years ago. This was who I was supposed to be. The people I was associating with were inspiring and optimistic. A few of my upline leaders in the MLM company brought me to trainings that were conducted by millionaires and tons of successful people. This started giving me a new perspective on wealth. I was infatuated with it all. I learned in these trainings how to let go of doubt and use my newly gained confidence for something positive.

It was now 2015. It was 9 years since 2006. I remember 2006 because it was the year I hit rock bottom. It was hard for me to believe so much time had passed, but I was finally starting to leave the past in the past and I was doing great. I started traveling more and went to a training seminar in Oklahoma and another one in Texas. When we drove to the trainings, instead of listening to the radio we listened to successful entrepreneurs like Grant Cardone and Gary Vaynerchuk on audiobooks and programmed our brains to be ambitious and inspired. At some of the trainings, we would hear the mention of God and someone saying they were grateful and owed it all to Him.

Listening to these professionals hit me in my heart and gave me fire. Because of the enthusiasm, it reminded me of when I would go to church youth camps. A part of me thought it was cheesy, but it was also a comforting feeling that brought me back to my inner child and inner self. I did my best to sell the products and ended up being one of the top recruiters in the state.

I had always felt like I was in a separate world from the majority of my peers, and now I felt so more than ever—only now in a good way. I was becoming an entrepreneur. I still had no idea what I was doing, but I was fired up about something.

I was involved with the MLM for about a year, but had trouble getting the business going. I was a top recruiter, but I couldn't get anyone in my downline to believe in what I believed in. Even though I was fired up, I was still a young businessman and didn't understand the disconnect between me and my downline. The disconnect lay in the *nature* of my passion: Even though I loved the products and loved the MLM business, I was hesitant in my belief in my ability to help others. I was fearful about what others thought about me and my selling of these products. In spite of my short-term success with the business, I slowly backed out.

Going Back to What I know

I had another passion elsewhere, and it soon became obvious what I should have been doing. I stepped back and reevaluated my goals, like that day in the sheet metal shop when I decided to become a personal trainer.

What in the world could I be an expert at? I'm already a Certified Personal Trainer; now I need a niche. So what could I be an expert at? Drugs! Fucking drug addiction. I felt more and more that I had a calling to work with drug addicts. My personal training was starting to pick up and I was more involved with that, as that was what was paying my bills. My drinking was down now to about once every 6 months. I still considered myself an alcoholic. I wanted to be the best at what I wanted to do. So if I were going to help other addicts, I decided I had to quit drinking. Total cessation of drinking came naturally and painlessly. I was ready.

I was doing tons of networking through LinkedIn, Facebook, and other social networking. I was doing one-on-one meetings with people weekly. I connected with a substantial group in Denver called Achieve Fitness Systems and landed a huge opportunity to build my business and build a bigger dream. I attended Achieve University, which was a 2-day-long seminar that educated me in how to build my personal training business into something more successful. I started out being a rookie entrepreneur and slowly but surely ended up as a polished and educated businessman, thanks to Robert Raymond, the CEO of Achieve Fitness Systems.

Through networking, I also connected with a corporate-wellness company. I had known the supervisor ever since I was a boy, and she hired me right away. This was a HUGE opportunity that came, once again, through networking. I wouldn't have found this any other way unless I had known someone to help me get my foot in the door. "It's not what you know, it's who you know." Believe that—especially coming from a felon like me, who is considered "unemployable" by many in our society!

The wellness company worked with a few large corporations, doing health screenings and health coaching with those corporations' employees who had health risk factors. This health-wellness company travelled throughout the United States, and it paid very well. My position was a contract job, which was perfect, as it allowed me to still make my own schedule and work my own business.

My life had literally turned 180 degrees within a year. Opportunity after opportunity began jumping at me. These were not always obvious opportunities; some of them came with the price of hard work and risks. The scary leaps of faith I took positioned me for success. I invested time and money in things that might fail. In life, taking risks was never a problem for me—another perk of being a crazy drug addict.

Recovery: Phase 1

Up to this point, there had been two big phases of change for me in my recovery. The first one was getting off drugs, learning to maintain a job, and doing whatever it took to say no to meth and heroin. I had to relearn how to walk, talk, think, and build a brand new me. Getting through the first phase was great, but I still learned a lot of hard lessons because I was young and emotionally immature. Not only the drugs, but the emotional trauma and psychosis had set me back and slowed my progress so much.

I still had a desire to be a bad boy during this phase, which almost landed me in more trouble, despite being clean, off drugs. A lot of the pain I had blocked out from my youth surfaced in this phase. All of the death and all of the things I had been through came to consciousness and were more overwhelming, in hindsight, than I would have expected. I see a lot of addicts and convicts get stuck in this phase of recovery. They get clean, they settle for a job they don't want, they settle for alcoholism, they are still angry or resentful. They choose to keep their feelings hidden, and they choose to endure unnecessary pain.

This manifests differently for everyone, but the bottom line is they are still giving up on their potential—settling for a lesser degree of success. They are called "dry drunks". They are obviously doing better because they are off of drugs or done with being *as* self-destructive. They may even go to AA frequently or do "good enough" at their jobs. But in general, they still embed negative perceptions and are somewhat toxic to be around, and they excuse it with the fact that they are not on drugs or alcohol anymore. This could easily have been the way I lived out the rest of my life. I could have continued drinking just on the weekends or getting into fights just every once in a while and been okay, because I wasn't on meth or heroin. I could have continued hanging around gang members and had one foot in the game and the other foot out—and I could have justified it to myself because I wasn't *completely* ruining my life.

My parents and friends wouldn't have doubted it much either, seeing that I wasn't *completely* self-destructive anymore and I wasn't killing myself with drugs. I could have done just enough to keep my family off my butt. I might never have gotten past that emotional block of feeling like I deserved less. But I pushed past that block and I pushed into another phase. I kept putting myself and my heart out there. I took smart, calculated risks and eventually it paid me back. This was my transition into another phase of sobriety.

Recovery: Phase 2

The second phase was my decision to quit drinking, change my attitude, and give up the bad-boy lifestyle all together. In this second phase, I chose to be optimistic and inspired.

I used to think being happy was cheesy. Or being encouraging was fake. Or that people who were like that were just sheltered from the nasty things that I had been through and were therefore naïve. I used to resent people who were successful. I thought those who thrived in society were just slaves to society. I thought I had to balance out being bad part of the time and being good sometimes. Why not choose to be good all the time? I'd had too much pride. I had to admit that I was wrong. I was wrong about success. After all of the drugs and after seeing all of the death, I was just uninspired.

A part of me had believed I was cursed by God Himself. It turns out there was beauty everywhere, all around me; I just never slowed down enough to look at it. I was also grateful for the hard times I had gone through because they taught me the value of my own life. Seeing all of these young souls around me pass, I realized I have only one life to live and that it could expire at any moment, so I had better give it my all and shoot for the stars.

I've gone through the wringer of toxic thought processes. I started out young and curious, but naïve. I grew into rebelliousness and ignorance, and in the previous years of my 20s I felt entitled and stubborn. Once I chose to be humbled, to be grateful, and then became driven, I started receiving the things I felt I had deserved my whole life. I realized that I deserved to have a good life despite my mistakes in the past.

Stepping into this next phase of grateful, humbled positivity strengthened my sobriety, too. For years, I felt I was unable to trust my intuition or take risks because, for so many years as a drug addict, my thinking had betrayed me. In the first phase of sobriety I did only what I was told by my probation officer, or my boss, because I believed, truly, that I was a crazed drug addict and had done so much damage in my life that I was not to be trusted with any big decision-making. Even in my own life! In my early sobriety, I needed that stability and mentorship.

But the time had come for me to grow out of that and move forward. I also learned that there was more to life than just *recovery* from drug addiction. That is a scary thought for any addict, especially in recovery.

I think this is one of the biggest separating factors between those stuck in the first phase and those stuck in the second phase. I witnessed these people in AA and around my workplaces all the time. Twenty years without drugs and alcohol, but still stuck on the fact that they are in recovery and unable to ever plan for the future or ever take control of their lives because they are an addict.

In my mind, I thought that if I started to let go of the past, or quit reminding myself that I was a drug addict, my addiction would somehow sneak up on me on an unsuspecting day and—BOOM!—I'm back in a smoke-filled room in a tweaker pad, shooting dope, coloring fuzzy posters, beating off uncontrollably, and ruining my life.

And, yes, that does happen to some if you disconnect from your dark self and over-celebrate your sobriety or overestimate your ability to stay clean too early in your sobriety. But, if done properly and slowly, and with help, you can start to process the past and then leave it where it belongs . . . in the past!!! You can look beyond and start living normally. You can set goals like a normal person. You can go to school, have relationships, and go to meetings. You can go beyond that, too. You can teach school, you can have a family, and you can be a leader in those meetings. There is a whole world outside of drug addiction and, yes, even outside of your recovery.

A fine line exists between what the system will tell you that you deserve and what you feel you deserve. When I was thrown into the system, on top of trying to manage an addiction that was killing me, I was expected to rise to the expectations of my probation officer and the judge—when I wasn't even able to rise to my *own* expectations. I wanted to die. The hoops an addict or a criminal has to jump through to pay a debt to society are frivolous to the addict and beneficial mostly to the monetary gains of the government. This creates spite. This created hate in me. I felt like my life wasn't worth trying to save because I was worth more if I continued dying from addiction. In active addiction, I can pay court fees, pay probation, pay for the parking meters in front of the court house, and pay restitution. The list goes on and on.

In an effort to balance this feeling of disproportion, I chose not to obey and to live outside the law. I had the delusion that somehow all of the bastard children of society would rise up with me and we would conquer the law and the system. That never happened. And although I believe the system is mistaken in its approach to helping drug addicts, I still had to accept more responsibility. No, the American system of treating drug addicts is not ideal, but when it's time to get clean you will do WHATEVER it takes to rid your life of drugs. I did what I had to do to get clean.

Another huge concept for me, which I'd heard about constantly in those training seminars, was to accept responsibility for my business. I translated this idea to myself. I realized that I didn't have to live as a victim anymore. All the times I had been to jail, all the needles I'd stuck in my arm, all of the robbing, and all of the violence and potentially life-threatening situations...those were *my* doings. All of the probation meetings and countless court dates. I couldn't blame the system forever. I didn't want those things to happen, but they did because I didn't take control. This was humbling and shattered the years-old chip on my shoulder.

There is a fine line between accepting that becoming an addict was *not* my fault and blaming myself for all of it. I did *not* choose to be an addict. I did not choose to give myself childhood trauma. I did not choose to have underactive brain chemistry. I did not choose for my friends to die. But while all of this wasn't my fault, it was still *my* responsibility to manage, and it was my job to accept responsibility for bad behavior while on drugs. Drug addiction is not black and white.

Without this concept I would not have been able to move forward with my own business or as an employee of a respectable corporate-wellness company. In the working world, mistakes are plenty, but there is no room for blaming others. Even if it is someone else's fault, I don't have the time to point the finger and complain about it. I pick up, handle my business, and move on.

Before all of these positive changes, something else had to change first. I had to forgive myself. In doing this, I began to believe in something greater than what I was settling for. After years of being convinced I was no good or that I was allowed to have only a limited amount of happiness and opportunity, I began to believe I was worth more. This started years back when I listened to the voice that told me "I'm worth more" or "I don't have to put up with this." Or when a boss would talk down to me and I believed that there had to be more positive people out there. I believed there must be a better way to lead. I was right. It took me a long time to find, but I did. Or I developed it myself.

In my health-coaching position for the corporate-wellness business, I found much more positivity and spark. Everyone smiled when they came in to work. When I messed up and made a mistake, the boss took me out to get coffee and to find solutions, instead of talking down to me and being degrading. I was given respect because I believed I deserved that respect. Also, in my own business, I vowed to be different and more positive than the others around me. I started doing little things to add charisma, like putting exclamation points at the end of my texts to my clients and colleagues. I wanted to stand out, and I wanted people to notice I wasn't bland or average.

I stayed out of comfort zones. Having to drag my mind out of psychosis time after time taught me to stay out of comfort zones. In psychosis especially, my conscious energy had sat in the deepest, darkest parts of my brain, where I wasn't bothered—where I could stay comfortable in addiction. Lingering in psychosis is strangely comforting when all that the outside world seems to offer is pain. When I was in psychosis, I could easily convince myself of anything, too. I could blame others; I could make up any irrational thought I wanted that kept me comfortable and kept me from facing my painful truths.

Despite what a chaotic life being a crazy person and a drug addict can be, all addicts get stuck in comfort zones very easily. They find the drugs soothing, and when they get clean it's natural for them to look for other things that sooth as well.

When the pain became unbearable and the drugs quit working, I used my psychosis to hide from fear. Now I cope with being uncomfortable, because I learned there is nothing to fear. Now I use fitness to sooth my problems, and find that it's okay to be comfortable sometimes—if it isn't destroying you. But in business and character growth, I make sure to stay out of comfort zones! Staying out of comfort zones is what causes my growth.

In doing business and striving for a higher success, I am constantly switching gears and finding new angles to attack my goals. In active addiction, I had no coping mechanisms for when I would have to switch my plans to accomplish goals. I would get my mind set on something I wanted, or a visual of how I thought things would go, and that comforted me. When things went differently, I would freak out, especially internally. I was living under the delusion that my brain had the best formula for success, and if something were to change it was always someone else's fault or a reason to quit. This thought process carried over into my early recovery and may have actually been worse at first with no drugs to suppress my frustrations.

Aspire to Go Higher

As time went on, working different jobs and enduring setbacks or complications, trying to finish probation or maintain relationships with others, I learned how to cope with being uncomfortable on some level. In my second phase in recovery, it got even better. This is still beneficial to my sobriety, because it keeps me thinking. I am constantly doing a moral inventory on myself. My perspectives are simultaneously changing with the routes I take to achieve my goals, and that keeps me on my toes.

It didn't occur to me until after a couple months of being an entrepreneur that I had learned some of these creative skills from the time when I used drugs. I had been somewhat fearless when it came to how I was going to get my drugs. I wasn't afraid to meet new people. I would go to the ends of the earth to get my drugs and, if I was selling drugs, I knew I had to make what I was doing look appealing.

Now I've eliminated the drugs and replaced desperation with inspiration, and I've found myself in the middle of some amazing successes and big projects that previously I had only dreamed could be possible. I've taken on some things I never thought were possible before, because I know what is possible now. I know that if I can come from being a worthless, beaten-down kid with a drug-riddled mind to a successful, in-shape, charismatic, and optimistic author and business owner, then I can go as far as I want to in life. I can earn six figures or I could earn a million. I can help people locally and I believe in time I will help people nationally, maybe even internationally. Nothing is holding me back except myself. And I've learned that I can use my hard background as a tool for fuel instead of setback.

When I decided to become an entrepreneur and chose my niche, I set two goals for myself. One was to write a book I had been planning to write ever since I endured the worst day of my life in 2006, when I was taken to the hospital and to detox. My mother sparked the idea in me a few days after the hospital incident.

"Ya know, Nate, with all you have been through, you should write a book to help others," she said.

It planted a seed. Writing had always been a passion of mine. In the last couple months before I dropped out of high school, the only classes I had any interest in were creative writing and English. I figured I was in such a deprived state of creativity and inspiration during those years that if I actually still enjoyed writing it must be something I was meant to do. During my junior year in high school, my creative writing teacher read a short story that had taken me about three hours to write one night when I was on meth. I turned it in, and when it was graded my teacher said, "If you hone this talent, you could eventually make money off of it." Well, here it is. Only this time I won't be writing any stories on meth. Inspiration and optimism are my new drugs of choice. Oh, and fitness.

My second goal has been to start something big to help drug addicts. I wasn't sure how I could do this at first, but in time I have developed a plan to make this happen, which can and will be achieved on many different levels. I've started a mentorship program, working with adolescents who are struggling with the law and struggling with substance abuse. I am also venturing out and trying to start an addiction treatment center.

These two goals are huge, and they are mine! I am thankful for every job I didn't get or every employer who laid me off, because without them I wouldn't have found my way to something that was so much better. I am thankful for the times when I am told no or I get shut down, because I will find another route and it will likely be a thousand times better.

I am thankful for my felonies, because without those I might have landed an average job and lived out the rest of my life doing something I really wasn't meant to do. Having my criminal record actually set me up perfectly to be an entrepreneur. The whole struggle of being an entrepreneur is a lot like my recovery: starting with nothing and building up.

In the drug game, I often would run out of money or a place to stay and have to get creative to find what I needed. Now I use the same concept with success. I use networking and meeting people, just like I did in the drug game, to get where I want to go. The only things that are different between finding drugs and building my business are the newfound optimism, the goal, and the self-discipline.

I was desperate for drugs and that's what made me work hard back then. I am still desperate, but for something else. I am desperate for more of myself and more life. I have only one life to live and I am desperate not to waste any more time. I am desperate to work hard so that my son can understand that anything is possible. I am desperate to prove to my family that I am more than a drug addict. I am desperate to prove that I am more than just a recovering addict, that I can beat the statistics and be more than the system said I would be. I am so desperate to keep moving, so that my mind stays busy and free from psychosis. I am desperate to prove that felonies don't have to hold you back from your dreams and to show others that you can start with nothing and end up with everything you ever wanted. I am still so desperate.

My Future

I am young with finding success, but very successful. The addiction treatment center is a dream in the works. It's just a matter of time. I know more ideas will arise as soon as I have accomplished my current goals. I will write more books. I will build more programs for convicts and drug addicts. I will continue to set an example for those who are lost in addiction, like I was or like my friends whose lives were cut short by addiction.

Success in the career field is great, but more importantly, my personal life is amazing! I have a fiancée, Christina, who is the kindest, most loving and most patient person I have ever known. My family has grown because of her, and the amount of love in my life is overwhelming and keeps me on track. Whenever I give advice, give love, give time, or give money, I am pouring it out of a cup that is everlastingly full because of the love and support I receive. For those who are hopeless and full of pain, thinking you will never find love, just hang on longer and believe! Focus on making yourself into the best you can be, and that is when you will find a meaningful relationship.

As for my son's mother and I, we have since made amends and get along great. She went through many challenges through the past few years including losing her brother. We have both made changes for the better of our families, and have now meshed our families together like one big crazy family.

I grow in my recovery every day. I learn things about myself that I never knew. I learn about my past, and I remember things I thought would have been blocked out for the rest of my life. It takes honesty with self and others. I still stumble in character daily, but I am victorious, triumphant.

I take pride in the fact that I am a little sick in the head. I think we all are, and that's what makes us different. We all struggle with our feelings and emotions. To deny those in yourself is to deny your humanity and restrain your soul, which was what drugs did to me for years.

I've blossomed into a person who is almost the exact opposite of who I used to be. If I feel that I'm falling backwards, I look inside and I see what's wrong and do the exact opposite or run directly toward my fears. I dig deeper and deeper daily to see what I can do to be a better me, because I know how devastating ignoring the inner me can be.

I get help from others, and they value my feelings and struggles, because I value my feelings and struggles first. They are real, valid feelings, and they are me. Leaving myself vulnerable also makes me strong. It leaves me open for constructive criticism from the right person, which can be life-saving and help me to grow.

Things have happened in my life that won't be forgotten, but that is no longer a curse. I am on a continuous learning curve from my past, and because I've gone through these things I have an edge in life that I think the majority of people in this world don't understand. That is my strength. My deep understanding of both the dark side and the good side of life is what makes me wiser and directs my intuition.

I still see tragedies today. Before it was all said and done I've lost more friends to diabetes, murder, more suicide and overdoses. To be honest, I've lost so many friends at this point I couldn't fit all of them in this book. Just a week before this book published I lost a former client and a friend of my fiancé's to a heroin overdose. The mental health epidemic in this country and even in my hometown is very real and persistent. I hope this book helps because I know what happens in recovery.

When a drug addict recovers, something magical happens. Another person is born inside of that person, a person who knows what it takes to survive. Someone who has had pent-up or misguided passion for years and starts to recover is able to do anything he or she wants, because he has known what it's like to live life with no boundaries.

Everyone, from all walks of life, has hardships in their lives and things in their past that they have trouble letting go of. I am here to tell you,

you don't have to let those define you. Stop punishing yourself for mistakes you made years ago. I don't care how bad they were. I don't care about your secrets. Tell someone. Be transparent and move on. Take responsibility, too. Accept what has happened in your life and move forward. No matter how bad it was, your life depends on it! Anything can happen. You can go from Zero to Hero.

Additional Support Groups

- **Al-Anon**
  Al Anon Group Family Headquarters: 1-800-356-9996
  http://al-anon.org/

  Friends and families of problem drinkers find understanding and support at Al-Anon and Alateen meetings.

- **Phoenix Multisport**
  Phoenix Multisport is a sober active community that welcomes those who are in recovery from substance abuse to activities that include rock climbing, yoga, strength training, boxing, cycling, running, and more.

  Located in Colorado Springs, Colorado; Denver, Colorado; Boston, Massachusetts; Orange County, California; and Boise, Idaho.

- **Alcoholics Anonymous**
  24/7 Hotline: (303)-322-4440
  www.aa.org

  AA is a 12-step program located in nearly every city. Easily accessible and a very welcoming environment.

- **AlaTeen**
  AlaTeen and AlAnonPhone #: 1-800-356-9996
  Alateen is part of Al-Anon Family Groups. Alateen is a fellowship of young Al-Anon members, usually teenagers, whose lives have been affected by someone else's drinking.

- **Narcotics Anonymous (NA)**
  PO Box 9999
  Van Nuys, California 91409
  Telephone: 1-818-773-9999
  Fax: 1-818-700-0700

  Narcotics Anonymous is a global, community-based organization with a multilingual and multicultural membership. NA was founded in 1953. Members hold nearly 67,000 meetings weekly in 139 countries.

- **Colorado Addiction Hotline**
  1-888-367-5749

- **SAMHSA (Substance Abuse and Mental Health Services Administration)**
  5600 Fishers Ln • Rockville, MD 20857
  1-877-SAMHSA-7 (1-877-726-4727)

- **Cocaine Help Line**
  1-800-COCAINE (1-800-262-2463)

- **Ecstasy Addiction**
  1-800-468-6933

- **Suicide Prevention Lifeline**
  1-800-273-TALK

- **Suicide & Crisis Hotline**
  1-800-999-999

- **Teen Helpline**
  1-800-400-0900

- **Sexual Assault Hotline**
  1-800-656-4673

- **Self-Injury**
  (NOT a crisis line. Info and referrals only.)
  1-800-DONT CUT (1-800-366-8288)

- **National Alliance on Mental Illness (NAMI)**
  1-800-950-NAMI (6264)
  Adolescent Suicide Hotline
  800-621-4000

References

- **Robert Raymond,** Achieve Systems Author & Mentor

- **Childhood trauma may cause drug addiction**

  http://www.narconon.org/blog/narconon/drug-addiction-may-come-from-troubled-childhood

- *Suicide Kings* **Script**

  http://www.springfieldspringfield.co.uk/movie_script.php?movie=suicide-kings

- **Love and Fear Diagram**

  https://www.drugabuse.gov/sites/default/files/images/soa_007_big.gif

- **What is the connection between fear and alcohol/ drug addiction?**

  https://www.quora.com/What-is-the-connection-between-fear-and-acohol-drug-addiction

- **Quotes about drug addiction**

  https://www.goodreads.com/quotes/tag/drug-addiction

  https://www.bing.com/search?q=quotes+from+drug+addiction&form=hdrsc1

About the Author:

- National Academy of Sports Medicine (NASM) Certified Personal Trainer (CPT)
- Associates Degree in Occupational Studies
- Owner of Elite Wellness, LLC
- Director of Elite Fitness Mentorship Program
- Corporate Wellness Health Coach
- Public Speaker
- Author of Facebook blog: *Addiction Recovery, Fitness, Love and Success*
- Member of Achieve Fitness Systems

Nate Wilson has spent the past 3 years fully engaged in personal training. Through his health-coaching, Nate helps corporate employees from all walks of life and he is devoted to showing those in need how to become healthier. His personal training business has grown steadily year after year.

Nate experienced a huge breakthrough when he discovered that he wanted to work with other addicts. Nate's huge passion is for helping addicts, both young and old, find their way to sobriety and then onward to successful lives.

Nate recently started a new mentorship program with youth in Woodland Park and El Paso County, Colorado, who are struggling with substance abuse and legal trouble. This program is growing, and Nate will soon run a larger program to help those struggling with addiction.

Thank you!

I would like to give a huge thank you to Joan and Tom for editing this book. It was a mess before it got to you guys. Thanks to Sara for making the cover look like something worth reading! Thanks to Raf for coming over and taking time to take the cover photo.

Thanks to Rob Raymond for guiding me towards success and keeping me on the ball. Thanks to my mother for giving me the inspiration years ago. Thanks to my father for raising me to be the man I am today. Thanks to my son, Solomon for being the star on the cover and for keeping me accountable day after day.

Thank you to all of my friends who supported me along the way even when I didn't believe in myself. Thanks to the lessons learned from those friends who passed away.

Thanks to my fiancé for being patient, supporting and creative with me and all of my crazy ideas and dreams. Thanks for not getting mad when I wake up in the middle of the night with a "mad scientist" moment.

Thanks to ALL of my friends and family!!